DATE DUE

OCT 2 2000			

Demco

GOLD RUSH SOJOURNERS
IN GREAT SALT LAKE CITY
1849 AND 1850

Volume Eighteen

University of Utah Publications in the American West
Under the Editorial Direction of the American West Center
S. Lyman Tyler, Director

GOLD RUSH SOJOURNERS
IN GREAT SALT LAKE CITY
1849 AND 1850

by

BRIGHAM D. MADSEN

UNIVERSITY OF UTAH PRESS
Salt Lake City, Utah

Copyright © 1983 University of Utah Press
Published in the United States of America
All Rights Reserved

Library of Congress Cataloging in Publication Data

Madsen, Brigham D.
    Gold Rush Sojourners in Great Salt Lake City, 1849
and 1850.
        Bibliography: p.
        Includes index.
        1. Salt Lake City (Utah)—History.   2. Salt Lake City
(Utah)—Social conditions.   3. Salt Lake City (Utah)
—Economic conditions.   4. Mormons—Utah—Salt Lake
City—History—19th century.   5. Overland journeys to
the Pacific.   6. California—Gold discoveries.   7. Gold
miners—West (U.S.)—History—19th century.   I. Title.
II. Series.
F834.S357M3   1983   979.2'25   83–12460
ISBN 0–87480–227–X

The paper in this book meets the standards for permanence and durability
established by the Committee on Production Guidelines for Book Longevity of
the Council on Library Resources.

To Everett L. Cooley, Friend and Colleague

CONTENTS

ILLUSTRATIONS

MAPS

PREFACE

W HEN the Mormon people settled down to a harsh existence in the Salt Lake Valley in 1847 after several years of persecution and deprivation in the Midwest, they had no warning that the discovery of gold in California would result in an invasion of their mountain home by thousands of gold-hungry emigrants. With the arrival of the first nomads into Salt Lake Valley in June of 1849, the Mormon people and these Gentile visitors began a two-year period of interaction that had a significant impact on the economy of Utah. This contact with outsiders publicized to the nation once again the peculiar marriage customs and strong theocratic control exercised by Brigham Young and the Mormon leaders in what was soon to be Utah Territory. This study will examine the mutually advantageous economic relationships that developed between the two groups and describe the social intermingling that took place as Saint and Gentile exchanged views, visited one another, and discovered common interests.

We shall follow the gold-rushers from the Missouri River jumping-off places, along the Overland Trail, where they met their first Mormons at ferries and trading posts, to their camps on the outskirts of Salt Lake City. At times it is necessary to differentiate between the events of 1849 and 1850, but generally it will be convenient to discuss developments at the Mormon Halfway House of Salt Lake City during the two-year gold rush period as a single unit. Following this general chronological arrangement, the study will examine the trading and bartering between residents and visitors, the division of emigrant companies into small groups of packers, the court processes and application of law necessary to settle emigrant differences, and the extensive social exchange between Saint and Gentile. After their stay of a week or so at the Mormon Mecca, we shall watch most of them depart from the valley by one of three routes to California, leaving a smaller group of Winter Mormons whose experiences will then be chronicled. By the summer of 1851 the gold rush was over and the flood of travelers through Salt Lake City was at an end until a family-oriented emigration began again in 1852.

Of the numerous gold rush diaries, most record the journey to California by way of Sublette Cutoff and Fort Hall or, later, by the Hudspeth Cutoff. Perhaps one third of the gold diggers chose to go by way of the Mormon capital. Of that number, some kept journals, and only a few of these diarists did more than record the weather. The staffs at the Henry E. Huntington Library, Bancroft Library at the University of California, and the Beinecke Rare Book and Manuscript Library at Yale University were most helpful in providing access to their treasures of diaries and journals. In Utah research took place in the archives of the Church of Jesus Christ of Latter-day Saints' Department of History, at the Utah State Historical Society, at Brigham Young University Library, and in Marriott Library of the University of Utah. I should like to thank the library staffs of these institutions for their gracious help.

In addition to emigrant journals, the four Utah libraries, of course, hold the diaries, journals, autobiographies, and reminiscences left by many indefatigable Mormon record keepers. I should like to express appreciation to my colleague, Dr. Davis Bitton, for his invaluable guide to *Mormon Diaries and Autobiographies*, without which a selection of materials pertinent to the subject of this study would have been very difficult. All students concerned with Mormon and Western History owe him a great debt. Access to the relevant Mormon journals has offered greater balance to the story of the gold rush through Salt Lake Valley.

Of the people who offered me guidance along the way in the production of this book, I owe special thanks to the staff of the University of Utah Press and to LaVon West for her usual superb typing job. Finally, I should like to express my appreciation to the University of Utah Research Committee for a grant that allowed me to visit the various libraries for research.

Brigham D. Madsen
University of Utah

O N the 16th of June, the gold diggers began to arrive here on their way to the gold regions of California; since which time our peaceful valley has appeared like the half-way house of the pilgrims to Mecca.

Epistle, Great Salt Lake City, July 20th, 1849; To Orson Hyde, and the Authorities of the Church in Potta-watamie County, Iowa. From Brigham Young, Heber C. Kimball, and Willard Richards. Millennial Star, *vol. 11, no. 22, Nov. 15, 1849, p. 337.*

GOLD RUSH SOJOURNERS
IN GREAT SALT LAKE CITY
1849 AND 1850

chapter one

SALT LAKE SETTLEMENT

A s the 4,200 Mormon pioneers of Salt Lake Valley looked out of their adobe and wagon-box homes in early 1849 at the first green shoots appearing along the ditch banks, they could give thanks that their isolation in the Great Basin gave them, at last, security from the mobbings and harassments that had been their lot for the last seventeen years. It was, of course, a reality that there were still several thousand church members living at Winter Quarters and other temporary settlements along the Missouri River awaiting the signal from Brigham Young to join the Saints in Zion, but that word would surely come soon.[1]

The twenty months that had passed since the first party entered the valley had not dimmed the searing memories of their brutal expulsion from Jackson County, Missouri; their forced migration to Daviess, Carroll, and Caldwell counties in the northern part of the state; and, above all, the massacre at Haun's Mill where over two hundred "militia" had cornered the remaining members of the thirty families of the settlement in an old blacksmith shop and had kept up an unceasing fire until seventeen lay dead, including a boy of nine because "nits will make lice." Gathering, finally, at Nauvoo in the more friendly state of Illinois, the members of the Church of Jesus Christ of Latter-day Saints soon witnessed a repetition of the Missouri persecutions, marked by an initial attack on Morley's Settlement, outside Nauvoo, where the Mormon residents were driven out of the village while a mob burned twenty-nine of their houses.

Some of the reasons for non-Mormon or Gentile hostility toward the Saints followed them to Utah later, so it is instructive to examine the roots of this opposition. First of all, the Mormon claim for continuous revelation from God, based on the Book of Mormon (part of the new record from heaven), was anathema to most orthodox Christian faiths. The Indians, or Lamanites, were viewed as recipients of special blessings, according to the Mormon Golden Bible, leading some to believe the Mormons were tampering with the Indians. Mormons were charged with proselyting among the lowest and most degraded classes of people. This made it easy for detractors to claim that these deluded neophytes, who were mostly from the northern areas of the nation, were determined to make war on slavery in the pro-South Missouri area. The Mormon people also maintained a rather solid political bloc, usually supporting one party in an attempt to defend their self-interests, to the dismay and resentment of the opposing faction. The Saints also tended to unite economically and to freeze out non-Mormon merchants. Their opponents, of course, could and did point out some of the extreme and bellicose public statements made by a few of the church leaders and the evident close-knit clannishness of the beleaguered Saints.

This composite picture of a nonconformist religious group with economic and political predilections, which seemed almost un-American to many in Illinois, led to the concerted anti-Mormon agitation that finally resulted in the murders of Joseph Smith and his brother and the expulsion of the Saints from Nauvoo. Under their new leader, the iron-willed and decisive Brigham Young, the Mormons began preparations, in late 1845, to move to a safe haven in the West. But any orderly withdrawal from Nauvoo became impossible under the constant badgering from surrounding Gentiles, and in February 1846 hundreds of families surrendered their valuable property for enough to purchase a team and a wagon. Loaded with only a few necessities, they crossed the Mississippi on the ice and streamed across Iowa to makeshift camps along the Missouri River. By the summer of 1846, the industrious and desperate emigrants had put in crops to try to sustain themselves during the coming winter while preparations were made to set out for a new home beyond the Rocky Mountains.

Then, in June, President James K. Polk granted a mixed blessing to the pioneers by approving the enlistment of five hundred Mormon men as soldiers in an expeditionary force to California. While Brigham Young endorsed the proposal, which eventually provided about seventy thousand dollars in wages and allowances from the soldiers to help outfit the wagon trains of the emigrants, the enlistment of the

Mormon Battalion left wives and children in the care of other Saints on the difficult journey to the Great Basin.

The oft-told tale of the trek of the first party of Mormons to their chosen "place" in Salt Lake Valley in July of 1847 need not be detailed here except to recognize that this mass movement of several thousand emigrants during the next year and a half remains one of the great achievements in American pioneering. The mild winter of 1847–48 in the valley and the absence of a concentration of antagonistic Indians in the area combined to ameliorate somewhat the rugged conditions of a first settlement. After three months of well-organized travel from the Missouri to Salt Lake, two thousand people settled overlooking the Great Salt Lake, a number which grew to double that within another year.

While families and friends were plowing and planting in their new mountain home, some Mormon Battalion members in California hired out to James W. Marshall at Sutter's Mill and were present when gold was discovered—an event that was to change American history and make Salt Lake City a crossroads of the West. Although rumors and unbelievable tales of rich deposits along California streams had filtered back to the East, it was left to James K. Polk, in his annual presidential message to Congress on December 5, 1848, to remove any doubts and assure people that the shiny metal was not just iron pyrite but was really and truly "gold, yellow, glittering gold."[2] Colonel Richard B. Mason, governor of California, had written the President confirming the verity of reports traveling east from the Pacific Coast. In explanation of his apparent delay in transmitting the exciting news, Mason wrote, "the reason is, that I could not bring myself to believe the reports that I heard of the wealth of the gold district until I visited it myself. I have no hesitation, now, in saying that there is more gold in the country drained by the Sacramento and San Joaquin rivers, than will pay the cost of the present war with Mexico a hundred times over."[3] No doubt as a down payment on the debt, the governor sent $3,900 in California gold samples which were soon on display in the War Department in Washington, D.C.[4] The *Boston Daily Times* extolled the virtues of Richard Mason: "Perhaps no public paper of our day has been more read than that of the worthy Governor, and we are not sure that he would not be an available candidate for the Presidency—provided the gold lasts."[5]

By late December it was "Ho! for California!" all over the East and Midwest. Extravagant claims of fortunes made overnight appeared in the newspapers. The *New York Tribune* announced official government reports that authenticated "Gold Found in Lumps of 16 and 26 Pounds!"; and it published letters from miners declaring, "At present the people are running over the country and picking it out of the earth here and there, just as a thousand hogs, let loose in a forest, would root up ground nuts."[6] One gold digger, Nathan Burr, reported that "another of the company lay on his belly and poked over the dirt with his knife and picked out gold at the rate of an ounce per minute."[7] The tremendous news was also broadcast to Europe. One New Yorker wrote to a friend in Birmingham, England, that "the amounts of gold are increasingly wonderful. Sometimes men have become worth ten thousand pounds, in as many weeks. One man out there has sent his father a barrel full of gold dust home, as a New Year present, reserving his cargo to bring with him."[8] The *Liverpool Mercury* of May 14, 1849, ran a special column under the title of "California" reporting such accounts as the miner who "never got less than 56 dollars, or more than 175 dollars per day." On March 16, 1849, the *New York Tribune* summed up the general feeling of the American people with the headline: "The Mines Inexhaustible."

Convinced of the wealth lying on the surface of California real estate waiting only to be picked up, men everywhere prepared to depart for the mines, easily ignoring various ministers of the Gospel who exhorted that the love of money was the root of all evil and that it was more blessed to give than to receive.[9] Advertisements flooded the newspapers with offerings of California Overcoats, John H. Stevens Matches, Edwards Celebrated Egg Powders, Mrs. Frazier's Compound Vegetable Cough Remedy, Indian Chologogue for fevers and ague, California Soap, California Ginger Bread, weapons of all types, and above all, such absolute necessities as Bruce's Hydro-Centrifugal, Chrysolyte, or California Gold-Finder and Leavenworth's patent gold washer.[10]

To ensure a safe passage across the continent, men banded together in companies to protect themselves from wild Indians and dangerous diseases. Some chose such fanciful names as the Buckeye Rovers, the Wolverine Rangers, the Hell-town Greasers, or the Colony Guards, but most chose more prosaic and business-like titles like the

Boston and Newton Joint Stock Association or the Granite State and California Mining and Trading Company.[11] Some carefully drew up constitutions and by-laws which were printed and distributed to each member of the company.[12]

By March 1849 the gold craze had reached its peak, as recently married twenty-three-year-old Adam Mercer Brown of Pittsburgh explained: "The yellow fever was upon us. . . . The magnificent placers of golden boulders in the mountains, and rivers of gold in the valleys—to say nothing of the lumps varying in size from a common tea kettle to a two-year old omnibus—had attractions for us. . . . The gold mania was raging. . . . There was nothing thought of but 'dig gold,' 'wash gold,' and grind quarts.' "[13] Only a dangerous journey by ship around the Horn or a long and fatiguing wagon trip across the plains and Rockies lay between fevered expectations of wealth and the actual reality of digging up twenty-five-pound lumps of gold. And even here there was a shortcut if you would venture to try Rufus Porter's "Aerial Locomotive" or "revoloidal spindle," a dirigible-type vessel 800 feet long that, for $200 one way, would transport you at a speed of 100 meters an hour in three days to your own special gold mine in California. Unfortunately, the dirigible never got off the ground.[14]

In Great Salt Lake, Daniel F. Miller thought that "the whole world seems in wild commotion moving on . . . to the Gold Placers in California";[15] however, some gold diggers began to send home sobering reports to the many "half prepaird frantick mad crasey or distracted" argonauts who had been exposed to a "world who with eager appetites Swallowed down every favourable tale of a few forthunate ones whose Stories lost nothing by being often told until they had increased the desire for gold in to a dreadful malady."[16] Instead of digging gold by shovelfuls in the streets of San Francisco, as chronicled by the *Liverpool Mercury* of July 13, 1849, the reality was that for one miner who prospered there were twenty more who barely made expenses. As the Mormon Hosea Stout tersely put it in September 1850, "Gold is growing scarce in the mines."[17] Nevertheless, enough momentum had developed to maintain the rush to California through 1850.

In the spring of 1849, the Mormon pioneers were more concerned with something to eat than in barometric reports on the fluctuating amounts of treasure being taken out of California streams. Most of the crops planted in early 1848 had been destroyed by frost and crickets, while fields planted later had been attacked by drought and frost and by cattle getting into the unfenced farms. In addition to the reduced supply of foodstuffs, an unusually severe New England winter, unlike the mild one of 1848, made the Saints' situation even more desperate. Beginning with the first of December, a solid freeze enveloped the valley until late February, with the coldest day plummeting the thermometer to thirty-three below zero. The warmest day of the three-month period was only twenty-one degrees above. At one time, snow fell to a depth of three feet on the valley floor, which made for scant fare for the cattle and difficulty in getting firewood from the mountains.[18]

Grain for making bread was very scarce. Zadok Judd thought he might purchase four or five bushels of wheat, but when the seller learned he was single, Judd was left to get his winter's bread from a sack of damp and musty corn but felt thankful for it.[19] By late spring there was "a great outcry for Bread."[20] When Aroet Hale tried to trade a horse, saddle, and bridle to the local miller for three pecks of cornmeal, the indignant merchant answered, "You great booby, trying to get three pecks of corn-meal when there are women here begging for two quarts to take home with them to feed their little children." Hale confided to his diary that the response hurt his feelings very badly, and when he thought of his own family at home without a spoonful of anything to eat of the breadstuff kind, he cried like a baby.[21] Most families did not taste bread at all.[22] As Joseph Robinson rejoiced, "A little piece of Johnny cake at that time was the sweetest cake I ever had tasted."[23] Mosiah Hancock's family was fortunate enough to have six bushels of wheat. They boiled and ate five bushels, and he ate the other one raw as he prepared his ten acres to plant his wheat crop. This diet was supplemented by some boiled hog when one of their two pigs was killed by the collapse of an adobe wall.[24]

In early February, the bishops of the nineteen wards in the city rationed "breadstuff" in the valley to three-fourths of a pound per day, a program that was to remain in effect until the wheat harvest in July.[25] Elizabeth Heward's family had to surrender three hundred pounds of wheat for distribution to the less fortunate, and she noted that the daily allotment was for each person over one year old, and none for those on the breast.[26] Appleton M. Harmon reckoned the ration as being "about 10 oz per hed per day until the Harvest."[27]

Their prophet, Brigham Young, came down hard on those who were reluctant to share their stores of food: "If those that have do not sell to those that have not, we will just take it & distribute among the Poors, & those that have & will not divide willingly may be thankful that their Heads are not found wallowing in the snow." Evidently this Old Testament sermon had its effect for loyal church member John D. Lee added, "Thus the reader may see the effect of the Preaching of the man of God."[28]

To the starving Saints who, like Benjamin Ashby, could record "I fainted away while following [the] plow," the prospect of ripened grain and garden vegetables by late June was like the proverbial manna from heaven.[29] This was particularly true of the appearance of the first vegetable—green peas. The diaries of Mormon pioneers and Gentile emigrants nearly always mentioned, with obvious delight and sharp remembrance, the diarists' first taste of that succulent garden delicacy. Wrote midwife Patty Sessions, on June 29, 1849, "Did not go to meeting we have green peas";[30] Hosea Stout recorded, "People are beginning to . . . eat peas";[31] and the *Deseret News* reported on June 29, 1850, "Elder Bullock married a couple on 16th inst., and supped on peas." One ungrateful gold digger, Finley McDiarmid of Wiota, Wisconsin, perhaps smarting from a five-dollar fine levied against him by a Mormon justice of the peace for cattle trespass, displayed his irritation by recording, "I hunted through the city for corn potatoes onions pease and beans. I found none but pease, and they were the size of No. 2 shot," which, he should have recognized, made them even more tender and delicious.[32]

The poor harvest of 1848 because of crickets and frost, the resulting hunger, the difficult winter, and the allure of a sunny California resplendent in yellow metal led to mutterings on the part of some that a terrible mistake had been made to settle in the desert. James S. Brown, one of the pioneers, described the feeling:

> In February and March there began to be some uneasiness over the prospects, and as the days grew warmer the gold fever attacked many so that they prepared to go to California. Some said they would go only to have a place for the rest of us; for they thought

Brigham Young too smart a man to try to establish a civilized colony in such a "God-forsaken country," as they called the valley. They further said that California was the natural country for the Saints; some had brought choice fruit pips and seed, but said they would not waste them by planting in a country like the Great Salt Lake Valley; others stated that they would not build a house in the valley, but would remain in their wagons, for certainly our leaders knew better than to attempt to make a stand in such a dry, worthless locality, and would be going on to California, Oregon or Vancouver's Island; still others said they would wait awhile before planting choice fruits, as it would not be long before they would return to Jackson County, Missouri.

This discouraging talk was not alone by persons who had no experience in farming and manufacturing, but by men who had made a success at their various avocations where they had been permitted to work in peace, before coming west. Good farmers said: "Why the wheat we grew here last year was so short that we had to pull it; the heads were not more than two inches long. Frost falls here every month in the year—enough to cut down all tender vegetation."[33]

A dozen or so families left or made preparations to leave for California in March[34] and one letter writer reported in April that "many of the tares have gone to the gold mines, and some of the wheat is probably gone with them."[35] Saints already in California and at the camps in Winter Quarters wondered about the wisdom of moving to the salt valley of the Great Basin, which mountain man Jim Bridger had already anathematized.

But Brigham Young, granite in his determination that "God has appointed this place for the gathering of his Saints," refused to be discouraged and would not be changed:

We have been kicked out of the frying-pan into the fire, out of the fire into the middle of the floor, and here we are and here we will stay. God . . . will temper the elements for the good of His Saints; He will rebuke the frost and the sterility of the soil, and the land shall become fruitful. Brethren, go to, now, and plant out your fruit seeds. . . . We have the finest climate, the best water, and the purest air that can be found on the earth; there is no healthier climate anywhere. . . . There is no other country that equals this; . . . we will cultivate the soil. . . . Brethren, plow your land and sow wheat, plant your potatoes. . . .

James S. Brown, who recorded this exhortation, added:

As the writer walked away from meeting that day, in company with some old and tried men, who had been mobbed and robbed, and driven from their homes, and whom he looked upon almost as pillars of the Church, one of them said he had passed through such and such trials in the past, but that that day, 1849, was the darkest he ever had seen in the Church. The thought of trying to settle this barren land, he said, was one of the greatest trials he had met.[36]

After almost two years of effort, the persevering Saints did what their prophet ordered and prepared to plant for another questionable harvest, not comprehending yet that the discovery of gold in California would change their lives and provide them with provisions and supplies which at that time could be obtained only in stores and markets thousands of miles away. The years of persecution in Missouri and Illinois had left a bitterness which had been only partially erased by the freedom of their mountain home—a brief surcease from troubling neighbors but in a land of desert and frost. The struggle to erect homes, to learn new methods of farming by irrigation, and to provide their own creature comforts far from civilization resulted in some grumbling. But for most, the news of golden treasure in California brought by returning Mormon Battalion soldiers was not alluring enough to dissuade them from building the Kingdom of God in the new Zion of the Great Basin. While the whole world seemed in motion toward the glittering rainbow on the Pacific slope, the Mormon people hunkered down next to their sea of salt and did their best to provide sustenance for themselves and for the hundreds of other church members and converts who would soon be joining them.

The years of being forced to move from county to county in Missouri and finally from Nauvoo had sharpened their knowledge of how to travel by wagon, what necessities to take with them, and, more importantly, what not to take. The tight discipline and careful organization imposed by Brigham Young and other leaders had ensured that the pioneers of 1847 and 1848 would successfully reach their new home with a minimum of privation despite the destitution of many of them. Their traveling hymn intoned:

> Come, come, ye Saints, no toil nor labor fear,
> But with joy wend your way;
> Tho hard to you this journey may appear,
> Grace shall be as your day. . . .

And should we die before our journey's through, . . .
With the just we shall dwell.

The wisdom gained from constant travel between Independence, Missouri, and the Great Salt Lake soon made the Mormons the premier plainsmen and wagon masters of the Oregon and Mormon trails. Brigham Young set the example by covering the distance three times himself while some veterans of the journey between the Rockies and the Missouri River soon came to know every creek and cranny of the Platte River road as they chaperoned new parties of Saints to Utah. With two years of experienced travel behind them and an oasis settlement at the Great Salt Lake, the Mormon people were in a unique position to help and to take advantage of the great transcontinental migration inaugurated by James Marshall's discovery at Sutter's Mill.

chapter two

MORMONS ALONG THE OVERLAND

THE throngs of gold seekers shopping the stores and corrals of the Missouri River towns for provisions and draft animals in March and April of 1849, contemplated the various routes across the plains touted by the published guides and rumors circulating on the streets and in the camps. Parties departing Council Bluffs had a well-marked road along the north side of the North Platte River to Fort Laramie where they crossed to the south side and joined the migration from St. Joseph, Independence, and Kansas which had passed through Fort Kearny. The combined companies were forced to cross the Platte again between Laramie and South Pass and then, beyond the Pass, had to decide whether to proceed on to Fort Bridger or take Sublette's Cutoff.

Sublette's Cutoff had been used first in 1844 when it was known as the Greenwood Cutoff. It left the original Oregon Trail northeast of present Farson, Wyoming, and rejoined the main route near Cokeville, Wyoming. About seventy to eighty miles of travel could be saved but, for the first time, the travelers encountered a fifty-mile desert that taxed to the limits the drawing power of oxen and mules and the patience and endurance of their masters. At the end of the cutoff the companies faced a dangerous crossing of Green River.[1] Nevertheless, an estimated two-thirds of the emigration preferred the Sublette bypass during the 1849 and 1850 seasons.[2]

For those who chose the original trail via Fort Bridger, there was a rather easy eighty-five-mile stretch on to Fort Hall with good grass forage along the way, but few of the forty-niners elected this road. Whether you chose Sublette's Cutoff or the traditional route to Fort Hall, another decision had to be made about three miles east of Soda Springs whether to continue on to Fort Hall or take the new Hudspeth's Cutoff which went directly west to intersect the California

Trail northwest of Great Salt Lake.[3] Most travelers took Hudspeth's Cutoff. For the one-third or more of the 25,000 emigrants of 1849 and one-third of the 50,000 gold seekers of 1850 who continued on from Fort Bridger along the Mormon Trail there were crossings of Green and Bear rivers and a difficult passage through the Wasatch Mountains, but the prospect of recuperation and new provisions in the City of the Saints was an enticement that attracted many.[4]

On the way west emigrants encountered Mormon travelers on the plains with whom they enjoyed amicable relationships. More particularly, they had business dealings with Mormon ferrymen whose services received mixed reviews. Earlier travelers to Oregon and California had profited from Mormon entrepreneurs in 1847 and 1848 who originally established ferries to cross their own people over western rivers but concluded also to make what they could from Gentile travelers. In fact, Brigham Young established the precedent of sending men from Salt Lake Valley each spring to take teams and wagons to assist other Saints in crossing the plains and with instructions to set up ferries at the Platte and Green rivers.[5] Lorenzo Sawyer noted that the Saints used a primitive "skiff of sole leather that would carry 1500 or 1800 pounds" to begin what came to be known as the Mormon Ferry on the upper crossing of the North Platte.[6] There was competition from the beginning from non-Mormon ferrymen, and in at least one early incident reported by Mormon Appleton M. Harmon the Saints tried to get rid of a rival by going downstream "to rekanorter the ferry below & see if it could be chartered for laramie post [i.e., cut adrift] . . . but returned about daylight having found it wellguarded & a faithful watch dog."[7]

Although the Mormon emigrants from the East usually started late enough so that they could ford the streams, their brethren in the ferry business had to come from Salt Lake early enough to catch the gold emigration. In 1849, Mormon ferrymen arrived at the upper crossing on May twenty-seventh and two days later carried the first travelers across the stream. By mid-June 1849 there were a number of makeshift ferries scattered along a twenty-five-mile stretch of the river below the more substantial Mormon Ferry, which kept its location at a spot three and a half miles east of present Casper, Wyoming. The Mormon crew just could not keep up with the press of business. As early as June 12, there were 120 teams backed up awaiting their turn to cross. The impatient emigrants who would not wait for the Mormon Ferry now set a pattern by manufacturing their own craft, which they sold to the next party who repeated the process, usually selling for the same price.[8]

Emigrant reaction to the kind of service which the Mormons gave their customers in crossing what James E. Squire of Rochester, New York, called the "miserable, dirty, shallow" North Platte during the high flood of travel in 1849 and 1850[9] was mostly favorable, although a few sharp criticisms were recorded about exorbitant rates. The ferry was substantial. It was composed of two dugout canoes on which a platform had been erected.[10] The most serious drawback was the necessity of having to swim the horses, mules, and oxen across the river. William G. Johnston, a literate, humorous, and quite descriptive observer, found the ferrymen to be "of respectable appearance, well informed, polite, and in every way agreeable."[11] D. Jagger found the Mormon ferrymen to be enterprising and obliging,[12] while Samuel F. McCoy was pleased to record that they were "accomodating and willing to favor us in all ways, contrary to the reports we had heard concerning their suspicious and churlish character."[13] When the Regiment of Mounted Rifles on their way to Oregon under command of Major Osborne Cross commandeered the ferry right in the middle of crossing an emigrant party, leaving two wagons on the bank, the patient Mormons took the two abandoned vehicles across that night arriving at 10:00 P.M.[14] The Mormon Ferry was much more reliable than the other float-by-night boats and there were fewer drownings at the crossing than at other points on the river.

In addition to ferriage, the Saints established a blacksmith shop with two forges to engage in repairing tires on wagons, to aid in cutting up wagon boxes to reduce loads, and, of course, to shoe draft animals, a process which cost from three to four dollars for a horse and six to eight dollars for an ox. The blacksmiths usually requested to be paid in bacon, flour, tea, coffee, or clothing, but accepted cash from emigrants on short rations.[15] They traded for lame cattle and could buy all kinds of goods and tools for a song.[16] The ferrymen also ran a makeshift store dealing in such goods as sugar at fifty cents a pound and whiskey at fifty cents a pint—any way to make an honest dollar.[17]

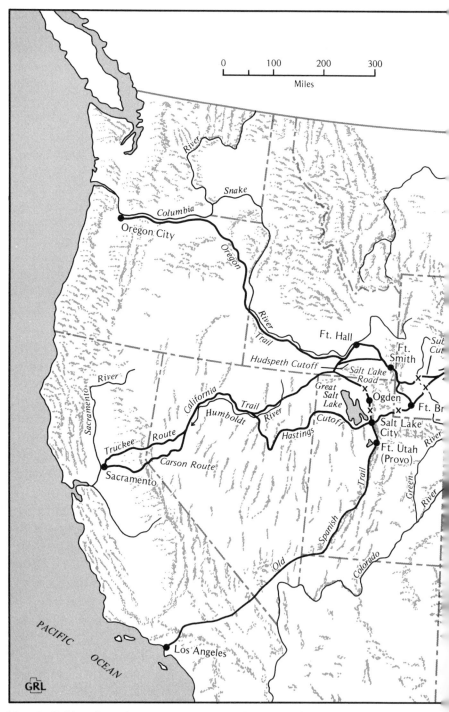

MAP 1. Gold seekers shopping the stores and corrals of the Missouri River towns could choose from several routes across the country touted by various guidebooks.

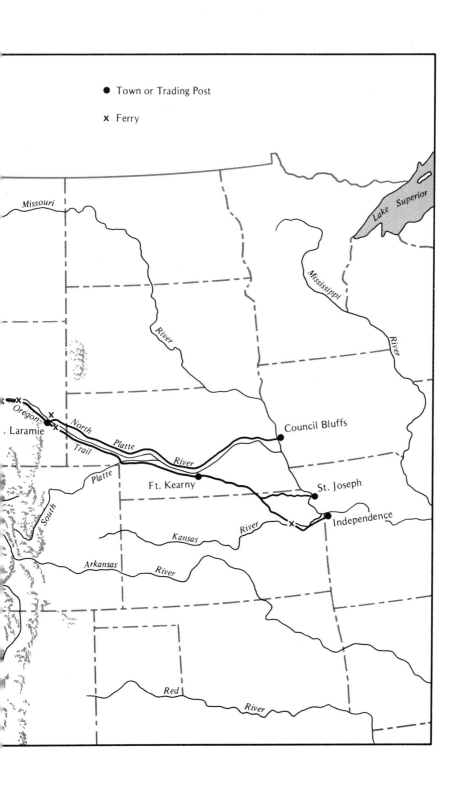

Town or Trading Post

x Ferry

Missouri

Lake Superior

Mississippi

River

River

River

x
Oregon
x
. Laramie **x**
North
Platte
River
Platte
Council Bluffs

South Platte
Ft. Kearny
St. Joseph
x
Independence

Kansas
River

Arkansas
River

Red
River

Despite the rather friendy business relations, there were instances of hostility between Saint and Gentile at river crossings. In one incident J. Goldsborough Bruff told two independent Mormon ferrymen who had the impudence to stop his wagon train "to be off, or I'd blow them to blazes."[18] On the other hand, Joel Terrill, a Mormon who ran a ferry on the Elk Horn River, was threatened by the Hawkeye Company of gold seekers who "with guns glistening with bayonets . . . ordered him under the pain of death to leave his raft, which he was compelled to do." The Hawkeyes had refused to pay the dollar per wagon charge asked by Terrill.[19] Generally, emigrant dissatisfaction was related to the amount of tolls charged. According to one estimate, an argonaut might pay $30 for ferriage costs to cross the western streams between the Missouri and the California gold mines. At the upper crossing of the Platte the Mormon operators charged an average of $3 per wagon, although they usually asked $4 to cross the army's heavy freight outfits.[20] Most emigrants did not grumble about the price, recognizing the extreme hazard of the dangerous streams, but at the same time they usually recorded the obvious profits being made. One observed that an average of sixty wagons a day were ferried over the river "for which they get $180.00. This I think is better than gold digging."[21] John Prichet commented, "They have as good a gold mine as any in California,"[22] and Doctor T. G. Caldwell wrote, "This is better than going to the 'Gold Diggings.' "[23] One traveler estimated that the operators would collect $250,000 during the seven weeks of operation of the ferry,[24] but Mormon John D. Lee was more realistic. When he visited the ferry in July 1849 the company had "met with Good Success, having made about $10,000."[25] Again, even his estimate may have been high. Appleton M. Harmon, one of the boatmen, reported a summer take of $6,465 for blacksmithing and the efforts of the ten-man boat crew.[26]

Of equal value to both parties were the two ferries operated by Salt Lake Mormons at the crossing of Green River on the road to Salt Lake, a river which William G. Johnston called the most formidable stream to be met with on the entire journey.[27] The nine-man crew included blacksmiths and wagonmakers who plied their trades and also dispensed meals.[28] Joseph P. Hamelin, Jr., of Lexington, Missouri, who had traveled ahead of his train on horseback to the Mormon capital, recorded, "They gave us a good breakfast of milk, butter, beans, coffee, mean bread & no meat—the first two mentioned articles were to us great luxuries."[29] The crossing was close enough to Salt Lake Valley that other Saints traveled there to buy provisions from emigrants, including bread, which was in short supply in the city.[30]

Charges for use of the Green River ferry started out at $5 per wagon, dropped to $4 when a Gentile went into competition, later went down to $3, and then, finally, to $2 near the end of the season when the river was fordable. At an average rate of $4 the Mormon operators may have made a profit of about $6,000 for the estimated 10,500 individuals and 1,500 wagons which crossed during the summer of 1849.[31] The next year, Charles Sperry recorded that the ferrymen received $900 each for their three months of work, and, in addition, they went out with nothing and came back with a good outfit.[32]

The operators at Green River received the same kind of response from their customers as did the Mormon ferrymen at the upper Platte crossing. Charles Darwin, quite verbose and mostly praiseworthy of his hosts, thought that despite the opportunities for gouging their customers, the Mormon operators were "perfect gentlemen . . . in conversation conduct and entire bearing" who did not "hesitate to carry any one for nothing who is poor. . . ."[33] On the other hand, L. Dow Stephens, whose travel experiences were told by himself in his own way, thought they had a regular gold mine,[34] and Joseph Hamelin made the sardonic observation that they allowed "our horses the privilege of swimming."[35]

But one criticism did come later in 1852 from John Riker's company which was charged $11 per team, or $88 for the entire train. Their captain refused to pay the exorbitant amount and offered $50 instead which resulted in the Mormon operators transporting all but one of the wagons over the river and then refusing to cross this last one until their asking price was paid. Faced by ten angry and armed men, the ferrymen were forced to produce their charter, which revealed that they were permitted to charge only $3 per team. The captain then drew his revolver and threatened instant death unless the last wagon was ferried over. The operators complied. Later, when a report of the incident reached Salt Lake City, an officer of the law was sent to Green River to investigate and the ferrymen were forced to refund the extra charges.[36] Brigham Young had established $3 for crossing wagons during the first year of Mormon travel in 1847 and that had been the standard scale ever since.[37] The 1849 and 1850 Mormon crews were evidently less grasping than their successors.

At the other ferry on Green River on Sublette Cutoff, the Mormon crew had to compete with some French Canadian voyageurs for the California-bound emigrants. Because of the competition, the prices for crossing at this point fluctuated vigorously during the season going from as low as $1.50 to as high as $10 during traffic jams that backed up wagon trains along the stream.[38] The Mormon crewmen had successful summers here during the two major years of the gold rush with what P. C. Tiffany called their "crazy . . . craft made of 5 canoes,"[39] hauling in as much as $250 a day and crossing over 2,000 wagons during 1849 alone, as reported by emigrant Amos Steck.[40] In addition, as at other crossings, they bought "broken down oxen at cheap rates and clothin which the emigrants are glad to sell"[41] and even engaged in friendly games of Monte, a Spanish game, with their rivals, the French rivermen, during which "a great deal of money was lost and won and I never saw before the cash pass away with so little grumbling, . . ." according to Steck.[42]

In addition to entrepreneurship at the various western ferries, some Mormon families also established themselves at the way stations along the Overland Trail to pick up whatever spare cash and trade bargains they could. One family set up a boarding house at Fort Kearny with such house specialties as buttermilk and gingerbread.[43] There were families of Saints at Fort Bridger and also at "Fort" Smith, a spot on Bear River near present Georgetown, Idaho, established as a trading post by Peg-leg Smith, an old mountaineer.[44] Associated with him was a family of Saints who traded in "lame cattle, moccasins; [and] whiskey piss," according to the indecorous language of John Edwin Banks.[45] And as the traveler reached Fort Hall, he would find several households of Mormons with "women and children who seemed to be happy and contented. They were evidently making money, for they had quite a large number of cows to milk, and between making butter and cheese and preparing meals for the emigrants they had enough to do."[46] From their dairy herd of forty cows, the women produced cheese and butter which sold for twenty-five cents per pound.[47] Milk was five cents a pint, and a lucky gold seeker might buy baked biscuits at four for twenty cents.[48] The families purchased rice, salt, and soap from David Swinson Maynard and sold him a quart of vinegar to help sharpen the taste of his bland trail food.[49]

A more obvious windfall from the gold rush for the Salt Lake Mormons were the abandoned goods left along the way by desperate emigrants who were forced to lighten their loads when their animals weakened under the strain of the rough roads. As emigrant H. S. Brown put it, "We were foolish enough to get everything under heaven that we did not want, and nothing that we did."[50] He and his companions started throwing things away the very first day of the journey and continued to do so until they reached the Rocky Mountains; that is, everything but some gold washers which they foolishly kept with them all the way to California. Many lost heart very easily and turned back, some going as far as Fort Kearny before giving up.[51] That post and Fort Laramie and Fort Hall soon became huge wayside dumps where almost any kind of article could be salvaged if you needed a spare part. One New Englander was appalled at the waste he observed at Fort Kearny: "It makes a man's heart sick. . . ."[52] While at Fort Hall, Joseph Wood saw Shoshoni Indian women visiting that dump every morning to pick up discarded items.[53]

Of all the many tales of emigrant improvidence, perhaps those of Captain Howard Stansbury and Mormon John D. Lee paint the sharpest pictures. Stansbury was on his way to make a survey of the Great Salt Lake and the surrounding region when on July 27, 1849, he wrote in his journal:

> Before halting to noon, we passed no less than eleven wagons that had been broken up, the spokes taken to make pack saddles, & the rest burnt & destroyed. The road is literally strewed with articles that have been thrown away. Bar iron crowbars, drills, augurs, chisels, axes, lead trunks, boxes, spades, ploughs, grind stones, bake ovens, stoves without number Cooking utensils of every kind, kegs barrels harness, clothing, beans & bacon many of which must have been very costly at home. . . . The carcases of 8 oxen which we passed this morning explains a part of the trouble . . . one of the men found a good rifle that had been thrown into the river. In the course of the day we saw 17 wagons which had been destroyed & counted 27 carcases of oxen that had died on the road.[54]

To profit from this waste a number of Mormons traveled along the Overland Trail from Fort Bridger as far east as Fort Laramie on what John D. Lee called a Picking up Expedition:

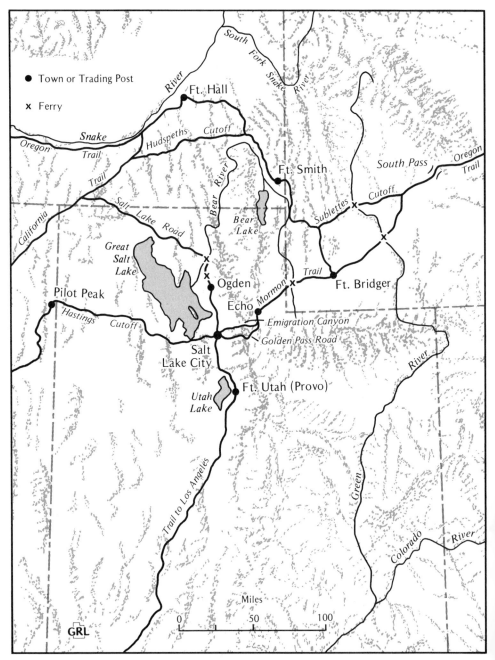

MAP 2. Pilgrims who chose the Utah route were swayed by news from mountain men, military officers, and other travelers that the grass was gone from the Oregon Trail and the Salt Lake Road was shorter.

The Road was lined with waggons from the Vally to this Point [Sweetwater River] that one would be scarcely ever out of Sight of Some Train. Dust verry disagreeable but not to compare with the stench from Dead carcases which lye along the Road, having died from Fatuge & Hunger. Distruction of Property along the Road was beyond discription.

By August 8, Lee was about thirty miles west of Devil's Gate, and he "commenced loading up with Powder, lead, cooking utensils, Tobacco, Nails, Sacks, Tools, Bacon, coffee, sugar, clothing & smawl Irons, some Trunks, Boot legs, axes, Harness, etc."[55] One observer wrote the *St. Louis Republican* on August 19 from Green River that he had counted about a thousand wagons burned or discarded and about five hundred dead oxen. He thought the wagons had been burned "for the apparent purpose of preventing them from being serviceable to anybody else. . . ."[56] The Mormon scavenging parties had a rich harvest in July and August of 1849.

To keep the neighboring Indians or anyone else from making use of the abandoned food, some of the emigrants who seemed to be born mean piled bacon like cordwood, poured turpentine on the stack, and set fire to it.[57] A more devious trick was to bury valuable goods in a grave with "a headboard on which was painted the name and age of the deceased, the time of his death, and the part of the country from which he came." So wrote Captain Stansbury of one grave which contained casks of brandy whose owner later sold them to some traders who received a carefully drawn map of the location of the grave.[58] Almon W. Babbitt, a Mormon agent, indicated that Mormon scavengers soon became aware of the strategem and "being somewhat inclined to marvelous deeds . . . gave resurrection to many bodies even before dissolution."[59] Sometimes, to avoid the exertion of gathering firewood, the emigrants just burned their surplus food or other flammable articles.

Some Mormon parties did not bother with the kind of goods which John D. Lee gathered but went after larger takes. One party of emigrant Saints found over one hundred head of oxen wandering over the prairie and, after checking ownership with the nearby military, added them to their teams.[60] James Mason Hutchings came across "some Mormons who were gathering up oxen [which] emigrants had left behind."[61]

Hutchings was one of the more interesting gold-rushers to visit Salt Lake City. An English cabinet maker who left for America in the spring of 1848, he settled at New Orleans as a newspaper journalist until leaving for the goldfields on May 19, 1849. When his party of five fell in with a group of army troops escorting John J. Wilson to Utah to be the Indian Agent and eventually to California where Wilson was also the new Naval Agent, Hutchings was hired by the army commander to be the carpenter for the expedition. He had a later career in California as a journalist and publisher, and his daily journal offers especially striking descriptions of trail life and of the City of the Saints.[62]

It was evident that the adventurers of 1850 had learned very little from their predecessors of the year before about outfitting properly for the dash across the plains. William Appleby of Salt Lake described how "Waggons, Harness, trunks, clothing, Beds, Bedding & other articles, with hundreds of horses, and thousands of Cattle lies strewd along the Roads and over the plains."[63] A brother Saint, Samuel K. Gifford, commented, "the horror that reigned in camps ahead of us cannot be described. Sometimes places for miles could be seen, feather beds, blankets, quilts and clothing of every kind strewed over the plains."[64] Mormon Nelson W. Whipple added his quaintly-spelled graphic description:

> The Distruction of property on the plains this year was *emence* . . . so many starting out that did not know anything what they needed on such a trip. . . . I am speaking of the jentiles—Wagons wagon irons wier guns chains beds shirts quilts pants tools of almost every description cags barrels etc. etc. etc. ware strued along in grate abundance I saw 12 Kiffel barriels in one place that had bin broken and bent and the stalks nockd of to prevent the Mormons from being benefited by them. . . .[65]

Joseph Fish also was of the opinion that the charred wagons he saw near Devil's Gate had been deliberately burned to prevent them from becoming Mormon property. But not everything could be destroyed and what couldn't be was, for a second year, "gathered up by the Saints and helped them very much," according to Fish.[66]

The determination of some emigrants to ensure that the Saints would not benefit from their misfortunes came partly from the widely held belief that the Mormons had adopted a deliberate policy of luring emigrants through Salt Lake City where they could take economic advantage of them. People from Missouri and Illinois also feared to go by way of the Utah capital because of past persecutions of the Mormons. For others, a decision had to be made when they reached the junction of the Fort Hall road. As was usual with the overland parties, they debated the issue, arguing the merits and disadvantages of the two routes with a common result being a split-up with some going to Fort Hall and the rest to Salt Lake City.[67]

Those who chose the Utah route were swayed by news from mountain men, military officers, and other travelers that the grass was gone from the Oregon Trail and that the Salt Lake road was shorter anyway.[68] It was reported that seven out of ten teams were going by way of Sublette's Cutoff and that "at least 3 thousand were ahead of us and no grass"[69] while only about three hundred wagons had gone along the Mormon Trail to Salt Lake City. Skeptical John A. Johnson predicted hard fare for these unfortunates,[70] but the ones who chose to visit the modern Mecca agreed with William Wilson, an 1850 traveler with a knack for misspelling almost everything. "When we left Foarte Bridger we expected to go what is calde Sublets Cutof but found the moste of the travle had wente that way, so we take the Salte Lake Rode. We founde the grass varey good."[71] Lieutenant John W. Gunnison, second in command of the Stansbury expedition, added his endorsement that the route through the Mormon settlements was the best across the country.[72] As for it being shorter than by Fort Hall, rumors persisted that anywhere from 150 to 250 miles could be saved, information which was quite inaccurate.[73] By October 1849, Mormon leader Wilford Woodruff wrote from Massachusetts that there were 500 wagons between South Pass and Fort Hall entirely helpless, the teams having died for want of grass, that the gold diggers were fighting and killing each other, and that an express rider had been sent from Fort Hall asking for help to get the destitute pilgrims to Salt Lake Valley to save them from sure death.[74] The report was highly exaggerated but confirmed the common belief that the Mormon Trail was the way to go.

Many emigrants, panic-stricken and fearful, sought help from anyone who appeared in a fringed buckskin jacket or whatever convinced them that they were in the presence of a real Westerner. John

D. Lee has left a good description of his meeting with emigrants in August of 1849:

> The general cry was, are you from the Mormon city or vally? Yes. What is the distance? Is there any feed by the way? What will be the chance to get fresh animals, Provisions, vegitables, Butter, cheese, etc. & could we winter in the vally? Do pray tell us all you can that will benefit us, for we are in great distress.[75]

It was not strange, therefore, that Salt Lakers, many of them traveling east to escort fellow members to Zion, passed along information about how good the road was and how plentiful the grass was on the way to the valley.[76]

Suspicious emigrants refused to seek information from Mormon travelers or else discounted it entirely. When mountain man Barney Ward offered to guide Joseph A. Stuart's party to Salt Lake Valley, stating that fresh animals and provisions could be obtained and warning that feed along the Humboldt had been burned by the Indians, the company at first voted to go with the Mormon guide. Then they decided to travel on to Peg-leg Smith's post to verify Ward's claim. There they discovered that the stories were false and took Hudspeth's Cutoff.[77] Bruff also "happened to be wide awake for these chaps," a group of Mormons who told him "lies, intended to beguile the emigrants down to the Salt Lake Settlement, where they might leave their wagons & oxen, for the benefit of the Mormons."[78] One company of gold seekers was so afraid of Mormon influence that the leaders refused to go near Salt Lake City; however, they lost one of their party when he was "induced . . . to leave us" by a Saint and his wife whom they met at a junction in the road.[79] Franklin Langworthy was "proof against any persuasion" by a Mormon to stay in Salt Lake Valley and successfully "escaped" from the settlement with the rest of his party.

The Reverend Langworthy was a Universalist preacher, a scientist, and a philosopher. His thoughtful journal, written in an impersonal style and finally published in 1855, is full of accurate scientific observations about life along the trail. He left his wife at their home in Mt. Carroll, Illinois, on April 1, 1850, to travel with eight other men to California. Along the way he seldom mentions his personal experiences or his traveling companions but does discourse in philosophical terms about the *Scenery of the Plains, Mountains and Mines,* a title that suggests his point of view. His only prejudice seemed to be his strong dislike of the Mormon church, and it colors every page of his chapter about conditions in Salt Lake City. The Saints could at least reflect that they were being condemned in graceful prose.[80]

The Utah leadership did not wholly favor the influx of Gentiles despite the evident economic benefits that came with them. When the first pioneers settled the Great Basin, their prophet had bluntly said, "We do not intend to have any trade or commerce with the gentile world," and the poor harvest of the first year supported the exclusion of strangers.[81] While the *New York Tribune* of March 20, 1849, could blithely advise emigrants that an "ample supply" of provisions could be purchased at Salt Lake City, the *Frontier Guardian* of April 4, 1849, warned gold diggers to take their necessary food supplies with them because there would be none at Salt Lake City, at least until after the summer harvest and after the greater part of the emigration had departed the valley. There was also the fear that the adventurers would infect the Saints with gold fever and induce many of them to depart for California.[82] Jim Bridger told one emigrant company that the Mormon leaders had asked him "to send all by Fort Hall but he told them he would not." The writer thought this was very selfish of the Saints.

In the summer and fall of 1850, Brigham Young was even more insistent that his followers preserve their provisions and grain. "You have no right to sell your flour to the emigrants, to feed horses and mules, and rob this people of their bread: What! sell bread to a man who is going to earn his one hundred and fifty dollars a day at the same price as you do to the poor laborer, who works hard for one dollar a day?" He advised his congregation to write their friends in the East and tell them to provide their own food supplies. There would be none for them in the Salt Lake Valley.[83] To help reinforce his dictum the *Deseret News*, on August 10, 1850, threatened to publish the names of the "defaulters" who had not heeded Young's wisdom. Later in the season travelers were forcefully advised to leave the valley and told not to make any plans to spend the winter there. About 1,000 remained anyway.[84]

In one sense, Prophet Young was inconsistent. Despite his warnings against sharing food supplies with the emigrants, he had already approved the organization of the Great Salt Lake Valley Carrying

Company, a Swiftsure Line, whose purpose was to transport passengers from the Missouri River via Salt Lake City to Sutter's Fort beginning in the spring of 1850. The fare would be $300 and freight would be carried at $250 per ton. The grand design never succeeded in carrying a single passenger or one pound of freight to the West, perhaps because the gold seekers supplied many of the products desired by the Saints. But church authorities were not averse to making a profit from the emigrants who would certainly have been involved in some purchases in Salt Lake City if the venture had gotten underway.[85]

Brigham Young's concerns about dividing food supplies were not shared by the California-bound excursionists who poured into Salt Lake Valley during 1849 and 1850. These travelers showed greater interest in the "slumpy and steep descent" from Weber River through the Wasatch Range to Great Salt Lake.[86] The road had first been carved out by the Donner Party in 1846. It led up East Canyon, over Big Mountain, down Mountain Dell Creek, over Little Mountain, and finally down Emigration Canyon.[87] General comments were devastating: "The most miserable road ever traveled by civilized man,"[88] and "The road through this Kanyon is certainly the worst on earth. . . . It baffles all description."[89] Nearly every diary included some reference to this roughest road yet—a surprise for the prairie-oriented pilgrims who were meeting their first real mountains.[90]

The road through East Canyon was so crooked that often the wagon driver could not see the lead cattle,[91] and the parties had to cross the stream thirteen times or "every half hour."[92] Ascending Big Mountain "over a horrible road over stumps, holes, rocks, logs etc.," the travelers had to "chain the wheels—drive carefully—get one or two men in the sideling places to hold on to the upper side. . . ."[93] The view from the top of Big Mountain was deceptive. Mary Medley and her family reached the summit of Big Mountain at four o'clock in the afternoon and decided that only a short journey would bring them into the valley, which they could see in the distance. At ten o'clock they were forced to make camp on the mountain grade at a place with insufficient room to pitch a tent.[94] The journey down Big Mountain could only be accomplished by taking off all the oxen but the wheelers, which were yoked to the wagon tongue, and locking all the wheels. Then the driver would slide his wagon down the mountain At Mountain Dell Creek at the bottom teamsters had to cross the stream twelve or so times in a distance of five miles. The road followed an easier grade over another hard hill, Little Mountain.

With a safe haven at Salt Lake City so close, the weary travelers now met the worst part of the trip from Weber River, the descent down Emigration Canyon. The creek had to be crossed anywhere from nineteen times (the usual figure included in the diaries) to the "*forty seven*" times recorded by Madison Berryman Moorman. This traveler, a cultured and "splendidly sane" twenty-six-year-old single man from Tennessee, left Nashville on April 27, 1850, as a member of the Havilah Company, a mining corporation made up of six outsiders, two Negroes "put in as cash stock," and thirteen white men. His journal excels in its descriptions of scenes and incidents. His picturesque accounts, bolstered by an extensive vocabulary and a cheerful sense of the incongruity of things, make his trail diary one of the most interesting to read. After spending five days in Salt Lake City, his party decided to take Hastings Cutoff to California.[95]

The crossings down Emigration Canyon were beyond description."[96] The descent resembled a huge flight of stairs, like Jacob's Ladder reaching from earth to heaven.[97] Locking the wheels of the wagon was not sufficient; most emigrants used the device of tying a tree to the hind axle to act as a drag.[98] Even then some wagons would be "slitely ingered," according to Simon Doyle.[99] Joseph Hamelin exploded, "The Scripture tells of a Devil, but today we had a combination of both in the shape of bad road, dust, upsetting wagons, breaking tongues, axle-trees, hounds, and other extras necessary to the further propelling of a wagon. Six overturned, scattering gin, brandy and other groceries. . . . What a regular spree the fish will have down below."[100] Finally "disembouging" from the narrow canyon, the worn-out emigrants saw spread before them the green fields and adobe houses of the City of the Saints.[101]

The way through the Wasatch Mountains was so bad that one Mormon entrepreneur, Parley P. Pratt, determined to build a new road through Big Canyon or Parleys Canyon as it came to be called. Brigham Young wrote in October 1849 that the new highway could be ready for the late emigration of that year—an overly optimistic forecast.[102] Pratt did not begin serious work until the early summer of 1850. He concentrated on the narrow and rocky lower end of the canyon, realizing that the rest of the route through Parley's Park and

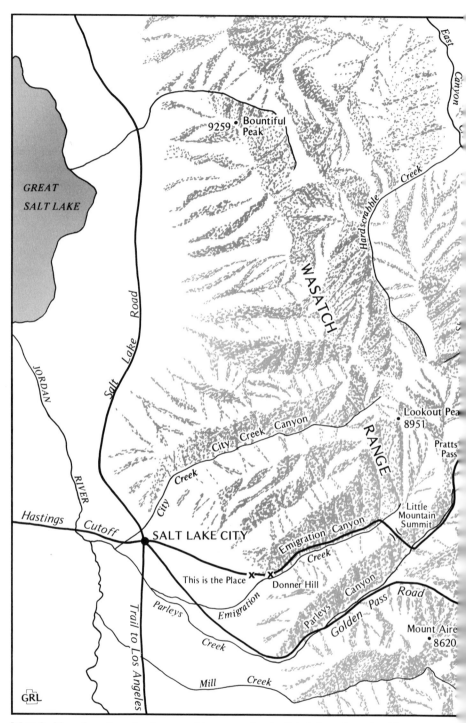

MAP 3. Travelers thought they would soon arrive in Salt Lake when they first glimpsed the valley from Pratts Pass—they quickly discovered the most difficult part of the journey was negotiating their wagons down the tortuous trail through Emigration Canyon.

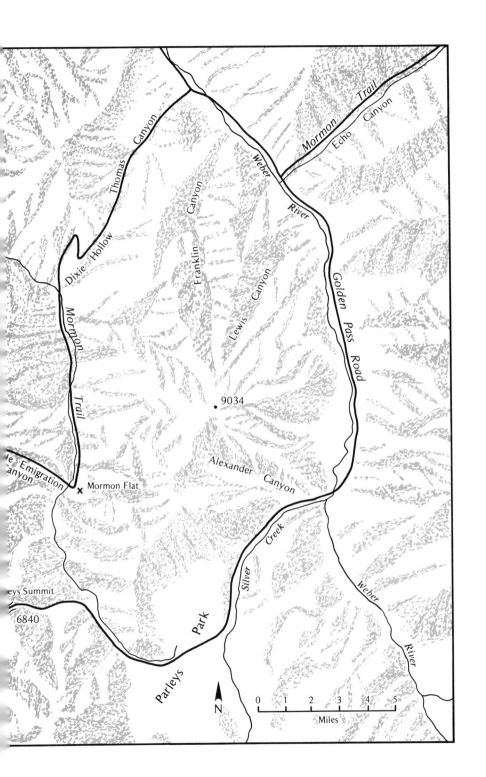

Mormon Trail

Thomas Canyon

Echo Canyon

Weber River

Dixie Hollow

Franklin Canyon

Lewis Canyon

Golden Pass Road

Mormon Trail

9034

le Emigration
Canyon

X Mormon Flat

Alexander Canyon

Silver Creek

Weber River

eys Summit

6840

Parleys Park

N

0   1   2   3   4   5

Miles

down Silver Fork to a connection with the old road on the Weber River forty miles away would be less difficult to construct.[103] John Pulsipher helped with the labor. He pointed out another advantage of the road in addition to garnering tolls—it opened up a good stand of timber for exploitation.[104] On June 29, 1850, Pratt advertised in the *Deseret News* that his Golden Pass road was open for business at a charge of seventy-five cents per conveyance drawn by two animals and ten cents per head for pack or saddle animals. He probably chose the name to appeal to the gold emigrants, whom he hoped would patronize the route.

The road was only in use one year, 1850, before Pratt sold it to raise money to go on a mission for the Mormon church. During that season the users were not very complimentary. The Newark Rangers of Kendall County, Illinois, the first company through, thought it was good, for a new road.[105] When Captain Stansbury led his expedition up the canyon on his way east after completing his survey work, he wrote on August 29 that the road was so crooked that he had to unhitch the lead oxen to get around the tight curves and had to unload the wagon twice during the journey.[106] Nelson Whipple, was not so restrained: "The road was almost impassable much worse we was told then the other way ... I was wet to my hips as I had to ... wade at every crossing which was not a few."[107] The new route was nine miles longer than the Emigration Canyon trail; it was difficult to keep in repair; and the emigrants reacted with hostility to the demand for tolls. Pratt did quite well. He collected $1,500, which relieved him of some of his embarrassments. As many as 5,000 to 6,000 emigrants may have entered Salt Lake valley via the Golden Pass road during the 1850 season.[108]

The journey across the plains gave many forty-niners their first opportunity to become acquainted with the Mormon people about whom they had heard many curious tales. Each spring Brigham Young dispatched experienced frontiersmen to establish ferries on the North Platte and Green River to aid Mormon emigrant parties and obtain profits from Gentile travelers. The ferrymen also set up miniature trading posts complete with blacksmith shops.

The emigrants bartered goods or paid fares for passage across the streams. They kept diaries that recorded an almost universal satisfaction with the services of the Mormon ferrymen. Occasional murmurings over ferry rates and prices at the blacksmith shops are counterbalanced by the many journal comments showing remarkable goodwill toward the Mormon operators despite the flood of business that often backed up traffic for several miles. The Saints did not raise prices for ferrying at the height of the season, heeding Brigham Young's warnings to retain the scale which he had set for them.

Special expeditions from Salt Lake profited by picking up items discarded from emigrants' heavily-laden wagons. These picking-up forays introduced other Saints to the Easterners, some of whom claimed that their new acquaintances attempted to steer the California-bound parties through Salt Lake City where they could be exploited. But most overland journals decry that supposition. In fact, by the summer of 1850, Brigham Young and other leaders were advising the emigrants to steer clear of Salt Lake Valley because of the shortage of foodstuffs and also because the Saints were beginning to tire of the legal squabbles imposed on their untried court system by the litigious travelers.

By the time the weary argonauts reached Weber River, they expected to arrive at the oasis of Salt Lake City within a day or two, not realizing that the most difficult part of the journey lay ahead. Negotiating the steep inclines and narrow, precipitous canyons of the Wasatch Mountains brought forth some of the most colorful and descriptive passages found in the overland journals. When the eager wayfarers finally reached the valley and saw the City of the Saints and the acres of green fields along the watercourses, it is easy to understand why many raised shouts of hosanna and thanksgiving.

The interaction between gold seekers and Mormons on the Overland Trail was mostly friendly and beneficial to both. The bad experiences in Missouri and Illinois darkened the perceptions of some Mormons and some Gentiles, but time and the exigencies of a difficult journey across the plains tended to ameliorate old feelings. The eastern emigrants looked forward to an opportunity for rest and reprovisioning at Salt Lake City, and residents prepared to welcome the newcomers and the possible trading goods that might be obtained to make frontier living less austere.

chapter three

CITY OF THE SAINTS

THE gold-rushers spilling out of Emigration Canyon in the summer of 1849 saw spread out before them a city of 6,000 to 7,000 people lodged in 500 houses, although this probably did not include the wagon boxes which some families called home.[1] Forty miles to the south there was a small, recently-settled outpost of about 150 people at Fort Utah. Forty miles north of the city twenty or thirty families lived at Brownsville and beyond the Ogden River. The Great Basin had no other significant settlements. In the fall of 1849 Brigham Young sent colonists to Sanpete Valley and to Tooele just south of Great Salt Lake.[2] About 1,400 new church members arrived during that year,[3] and perhaps 2,500 came during the emigrating season of 1850. By the time of the official 1850 census count, with the addition of some temporary Gentile citizens, there were 11,380 people in Utah Territory; about 8,000 were in Salt Lake Valley, including 26 slaves and 24 "free colored."[4]

Estimates of the number of adventurers who poured through the City of the Saints during the first two years of the gold rush vary from 10,000 for 1849 to 15,000 for 1850.[5] Brigham Young recorded in late September 1850 that "their number has been much larger than the previous year."[6] At the height of the influx of emigrants in 1850, one company was held up for two hours in Emigration Canyon because of the accumulation of teams on the road. When they finally stopped for the night in the valley they found immense numbers of emigrants encamped.[7] The flood of California-bound travelers in 1850 was so great in the valley and on the Salt Lake Road north of the city that Brigham Young cancelled sending a group of missionaries to the Society Islands fearing that their journey to the Pacific Coast would be too hazardous.[8]

[33]

The first excursionists of 1849 arrived on June 16.[9] According to Charles D. Ferguson, the first company of 1850 arrived May 19, much to the surprise of the Saints who had not expected travelers so early. Ferguson's party had covered the 1,300 miles from St. Louis in a record-breaking forty-nine days. Ferguson had left Ohio at the age of seventeen to live with a brother in Ottawa, Illinois, and the following year, on March 14, 1850, he and three other townspeople left for the plains and gold diggings. While his journal has a down-to-earth quality, it also reveals the diarist as a fairly well-educated young man with a sense of humor and an eye for interesting detail.[10]

A more usual trip was one carefully described by Amos Piatt Josselyn in 1849 in a letter to his wife in Zanesville, Ohio. He traveled 1,177 miles from Independence in 82 days, with 62½ days of actual travel time and 19½ days which were lost en route.[11] A number of diaries by Mormons and Gentiles record the interesting fact that several hundred emigrants reached Salt Lake on July twenty-fourth, the date on which Brigham Young and his party had first entered the valley. The *Deseret News*, started in June of 1850, offered to print the names, home addresses, and arrival and departure dates of those emigrants who were willing to pay twenty-five cents for the service, which included sending a copy of the paper to anyone in the states designated by the traveler.[12] An examination of the over 600 names printed reveals that the average stay in Salt Lake City was 6½ days with some gold seekers staying as long as five weeks and fewer stopping for only a day before rushing on to their fortunes on the American River.[13] The Mormon capital was a very important recruiting station for these overland pilgrims.

Many emigrants recorded their reactions to their first view of Salt Lake Valley after two or three months of travel on the dusty plains. One man in the Buckeye Company described it as "the most wonderful sight so far seen in our travels. For a moment not a word came from a single member of the company—all were speechless at the grand scenery before us—when of a sudden the members of the Buckeye Camp yelled at the top of their voices."[14] A *New York Tribune* correspondent wrote from Salt Lake City on October 9, 1849, "At first sight of all these signs of cultivation in the wilderness, we were transported with wonder and pleasure. Some wept, some gave three cheers, some laughed, and some ran and fairly danced for joy.

. . ."[15] Numerous accounts describe the travelers' exhilaration.[16] Some were astonished to see an old, settled country in the wilderness.[17]

However, Langworthy, following his usual condemnation of anything Mormon, was disappointed to find a "neighborhood of farmers and mechanics" rather than a city.[18] One newcomer, H. S. Beatie, who was soon to join the Mormon church, groused that if he "had ever struck a country town I did when I struck Salt Lake."[19] Captain Stansbury was more diplomatic. He suggested that after some shade trees had been planted the place would become one of the loveliest spots between the Mississippi and the Pacific Coast, a "Diamond of the Desert."[20]

Englishman William Kelly was openly hostile to the "bald, level plain . . . without bush or bramble to cast a shade" on which Salt Lake City was located. Of all the emigrant diaries examined, Kelly's has a special quality because he took a rather lofty and bemused look at the events and people he encountered on the trail. As he wrote in the preface to *An Excursion to California*, he adopted a "light style of writing . . . in expectation that perhaps the humor may countervail the lack of higher attributes. . . ." He was quite well-educated and evidently a person of substance. His plains company (made up of eight Yankees, two Scotchmen, two Irishmen, and thirteen Englishmen) elected him captain as they left Independence on April 16, 1849, bound for the treasures of California. His writing sparkles with sprightly comments and interesting descriptions.[21]

W. S. McBride, late of Goshen, Indiana, expected to see the Mormon settlement "shine forth *bright, prominent & conspicuous* city-like; and hence we looked too high & too far away. If we had looked low down close to the earth with a steady gaze we might have beheld a large group of small dark objects which afterwards proved to be mud houses or hovels."[22]

After recovering from their initial reactions to the panorama of a city in the wilderness, the gold emigrants began to record in their diaries descriptions of picturesque details of the new settlement. They marveled at the surrounding mountains covered with perpetual snow despite the quite warm temperatures in the valley below.

The most striking characteristic of the "verry Pretty" city to many were the magnificent distances and the very scattered appearance of a town which was not compactly built.[24] Stansbury thought that the place had been laid out upon a magnificent scale—four miles in length and three wide, with streets at right angles and 132 feet wide and sidewalks 20-feet wide. The blocks, forty rods square, were divided into eight lots, each with an acre and a quarter of ground.[25] Brigham Young had explained to his followers that the houses were to be set twenty feet back from the street "with no shops or other buildings" on the street corners.[26] An emigrant noted one result of the plan—"All was quiet." There were no vehicles to create noise.[27] Silas Newcomb, who had started from Darien, Wisconsin, "for the Gold Region (Calif.) or Oregon as circumstances feelings dictate," explained that there were 171 blocks of 10 acres each, with 19 ecclesiastical wards, each containing 9 blocks or 90 acres— altogether 1,710 acres.[28] Simon Doyle, was intrigued by the novel arrangement of the dwellings. "The plan is such that when each lot in the city has its building erected upon it the doors of no two houses shut from each other."[29]

The city lots were awarded by tickets bearing the numbers of the acreage being drawn from a hat, according to one interested Gentile.[30] Good Mormon Nelson Whipple gave a more accurate description. He was told to apply to Brigham Young's first counselor, Heber C. Kimball, who met each Saturday with interested parties and gave "of the lots to each one as it seemed him good. . . ." Then, by paying $1.50 for surveying and recording costs, each person received ownership. Whipple found his lot half covered with water and then just squatted on a drier lot until he secured title to it.[31]

John Hudson, a young gold-rusher from England, was amazed that for $1.50 he could become the owner of one and a quarter acres of ground on which he could produce sufficient food for a year for himself. Hudson, a twenty-one-year-old artist and second son of a well-to-do family in Birmingham, England, had gone to New York to act as agent for his uncle's import-export business but left for the gold fields when a slight recession dampened his prospects. Joining with twenty-four other New York "gentlemen," they formed a gold-seeking corporation called the Colony Guard and started across the plains. Hudson almost died of the cholera and was forced to remain in Salt Lake City while his companions went on to California. In the spring of 1850 he was hired by Howard Stansbury to be the artist for the exploring party that surveyed Great Salt Lake.[32]

In addition to the city lot that single individuals like Hudson could obtain, men with families were assigned farms of twenty acres or more outside the city, the size depending on the number in the family and the owner's ability to cultivate the land.[33] Of course, it was understood by orders from Brigham Young that no one was allowed to cut up his lot and sell it for a speculative profit. In numerous sermons, Brigham Young also reprimanded slothful individuals and warned that if they did not improve their land they would be deprived of their lots and be expelled from Zion.[34]

The habitations of those who received allotments in the city were primitive indeed—log cabins, wagon boxes,[35] "or just a few pieces of lumber set end-ways and coming together at the top, with a sheet fastened across each end . . . for a door."[36] The most common structure was built of adobes or sun-burnt brick,[37] with dirt or gravel roofs because the only available wood was in the nearby canyons ten or twelve miles away, a distance which required a two-day journey to procure a load.[38] The adobes were twelve inches long, six inches wide, and twenty-one inches thick. They made very comfortable dwellings —cool in summer, warm in winter. The builders projected the eaves to protect the walls from rain and snow.[39] Adobe buildings gave the appearance from a distance of being painted a lead gray or a "mortar colour (if that can be defined)," as Charles Glass Gray put it. Gray was a traveler from Newark, New Jersey. His journal is filled with the exact miles covered, the 164 camps made by his party, and careful descriptions of the weather. During his five days in Salt Lake City he enjoyed the bounteous food served by his Mormon hosts but thought that there "appears to be a tinge of fanaticism as it were about their customs, their looks & manners."[40] Although James Squire thought the adobe houses made the city look like "a settlement of Irishmen around some public works,"[41] most agreed that the houses were neat looking and that the color was very pleasing.[42]

Emigrant diaries or letters usually mentioned the only public buildings in Salt Lake—a Council House, also constructed of adobes but of an imposing two stories, and the much-used Bowery, or temporary tabernacle. On July 1, 1849, Brigham Young ordered the construction of a public meeting house or "shade of boards," to be ready for the first major Pioneer Day celebration on July twenty-fourth.[43] The local militia, the Nauvoo Legion, laid down their weapons and, with pick and spade, prepared the foundations and then helped to build the adobe walls and erect the pilasters, beams, and roof of the 100 by 60 foot structure.[44] It was a primitive affair "built by setting posts in the ground and sided up with willow poles from one to two inches thru, reaching to the eaves; then tying them at top and bottom with bark. Then small willows over the top covered with 'dust' constituted the roof."[45] The benches were of rough-sawed lumber as was the pulpit, with "no pains being made to plane the boards."[46] The Bowery held up to two thousand people if you counted those who sat in their parked wagons in the rear of the drive-in church.[47] The building was used almost every evening in addition to Sabbath meetings "to teach, counsel, and devise ways and means for the prosperity of the Kingdom of God. . . ."[48] Just next to the Bowery could be seen the foundations of the proposed Temple, a building of stupendous proportions.[49] Gold seeker Simon Doyle learned that it would be "the Most Magnificent structure now on the earth so sais some of the Lady Saints with whom I conversed upon the subject."[50]

The emigrants from the East were particularly fascinated by the valley's irrigation system which diverted the streams from several Wasatch canyons to the inclined plane leading down to the Jordan River. William Kelly, accustomed to a green and well-sprinkled country, rather dryly observed, "as there is little or no rain in this region, a Salt Lake shower . . . [is] estimated at a drop to each inhabitant."[51] Jerome B. Howard detailed for his hometown newspaper how irrigation worked, noting that the furrows which carried the rivulets were a little lower than the surface of the water and when the farmer wanted to irrigate, usually once a week, "a communication is made with a shovel, between the stream and each furrow." In three long letters from Bidwell's Bar on the Feather River to the Marietta, Ohio, *Intelligencer*, Howard told of his experiences as an overland traveler (by way of the Arkansas River and Utah Valley) and as a miner in California. The first letter dealt with his three-week stay in Salt Lake Valley. He described in excellent prose the physical, economic, governmental, and social aspects of the new Mormon settlement. He was thorough and objective in his evaluation and endeavored to present the Saints in as fair and impartial a light as possible. He succeeded fairly well and has left to posterity one of the best accounts of Mormon life and culture during the gold rush period.[52]

The twenty miles of ditch around the city, which comprised the valley irrigation system, distributed through small artificial ducts the cool, pure, clear, and delightful mountain water. The water flowed at the rate of four knots an hour, a velocity that created such a rushing sound it could be heard in all sections of the city.[54] The streams on each side of a street carried water to the doorsteps of the houses where it was used for culinary purposes and to irrigate the vegetable crops and fruit trees in this City of Gardens,[55] "spreading life, verdure, and beauty over what was heretofore a barren waste."[56]

Outside the city lay the farming area for which Brigham Young had devised a master plan in September 1848. A main irrigation canal was plotted to run from Big Cottonwood Creek north along the foot of the mountains. Just below the large ditch[57] a common Big Field, three miles wide and fourteen miles long, was separated from the pasture lands to the south by an east-west pole fence seventeen miles in length and eight feet high.[58] The field thus enclosed a very large amount of land; it was divided into five- and ten-acre plots awarded by lot to an initial 900 applicants.[59] There were other farms south of the main field scattered within the common grazing area. The owners were responsible for fencing these larger acreages. One emigrant noted in 1850 that other plans envisioned another Big Field to be enclosed north of the city in what is now the Bountiful area. When one group of gold seekers saw the large field full of waving grain in July 1849, John B. Hazlip, of Palmyra, Missouri, who had just recovered from a bout of mountain fever, was so impressed he thought there must be at least 50,000 acres of wheat in sight.[60] Henry S. Bloom more correctly estimated 25,000 acres in 1850.[61]

At planting time, in the spring of 1849, the scantily-provisioned Saints probably shared fervent William Greenwood's hope for a good harvest, "I dedicated the seed and the ground to Gods trusting in him for the increase. . . ."[62] And emigrant journals, with only a few demurrers, testified that his prayer was answered. With the exception of corn, which most thought "looked weak and sickly and verry backward" because of bad frosts,[63] magnificent crops of wheat, oats, and barley were observed in both gold rush years. One traveler described stalks of wheat seven feet high bearing large, full heads.[64] The yields impressed most viewers.[65] Stansbury and at least one other, Isaac C. Haight, reported 180 bushels of wheat raised from one bushel of seed "which beats the world."[66] The amount of the wheat harvest estimated by the Gentile observers varied from 30 bushels per acre to the extravagant claim of 100 bushels by Joseph Summers, with most rather evenly divided between approximations of 50 bushels and 80 bushels per acre.[67] A few detractors agreed with Finley McDiarmid that the wheat was poor and the gardens unfruitful.[68]

Whatever the correct amount, the harvest of 1849 was large and greatly welcomed by both Saint and Gentile. One traveler noted in 1849 that "the folks here will have a poor chance of starving this year."[69] William B. Lorton, a painter from New York who lost all he owned on his journey to Los Angeles, expected that the Mormon people would have a thousand bushels of surplus grain "but do not throw out inducements to emigrants,"[70] Jerome Howard, however, was sure the overlanders could purchase all they wanted.[71] When Joseph Summers deprecated a poor looking stand of wheat, he was informed it was the second crop which even then would probably produce thirty bushels per acre.[72] Reports circulated that the Mormons had raised three crops,[73] which only enforced Stansbury's judgment of the "prodigious productiveness" of the soil which yielded a superior quality of grain.[74] There were so many acres under cultivation in 1850 that Brigham Young expressed thankfulness for the above-average summer rainfall which lessened the need for irrigation with his depleted labor force of farmers.[75] The harvest of 1849 was estimated at 130,000 bushels of cereals[76] while the 1850 census listed 128,711 bushels of grain grown in Salt Lake Valley.[77]

The census also revealed that the Mormon pioneers were well provided with oxen, horses, and other stock, a fortunate circumstance for the overlanders who could trade their weakened and worn-out draft animals for fresh ones in Salt Lake City. The government tables showed totals for Utah Territory of 5,266 working oxen, 2,429 horses, 325 mules, 4,861 milch cows, 2,489 other cattle, 3,262 sheep, and 914 swine.[78] Cattle were kept on the range all winter. Rangeland furnished "the Best grazing here now that I have ever seen in any Place," according to William Kilgore.[79] The commonly-owned pasture, particularly northwest of the city toward the river, was the favorite grazing area, although some residents drove their cattle "beyond

Jordan" during the day returning them to corrals at night.[80] The tremendous influx of emigrants during the two gold rush years soon depleted the available forage near the city, and newcomers were forced to set up camp to the west by the Jordan River where grass was not so short.[81] The Mormon leaders finally had to insist, gently but firmly, that the travelers move some distance away from the city to ensure grazing for local stock and to stop Gentile horses and oxen from breaking into the grain fields.[82]

Protecting the precious grain was paramount during the early years in Salt Lake Valley, and most emigrants were regaled, in sermon or in private conversation, with the "cricket miracle" account of the difficult summer of 1848.[83] As loyal Saint George Morris told the story, hordes of black crickets came into the fields to devour the precious crops; at the last moment, flocks of seagulls appeared from Great Salt Lake to devour the insects; and "so with what the Lord had done for us with the gulls and what we done for ourselves," the pioneers were saved from starvation.[84] Daniel Spencer, like most thankful pioneers, had no patience with "sarcastic infidelic statements" that the gulls had been in the area for years before the coming of the Mormons and that they ate the crickets by instinct.[85] Nevertheless, the crisis had been so serious that orders had gone out to the people to save their teams and wagons "for we might need them," apparently to move on to California.[86]

In 1849, emigrants as well as Saints were able to observe the ravages of crickets and to watch the farmers' attempts to kill the insects by drowning them with irrigation water or by massacring them with "light Mauls or Mallettes." Again, the sea birds "repulsed the Destroyers," in the words of John D. Lee.[87] Crickets ravaged crops much less in 1849 and 1850 than in 1848, and some of the literate emigrant cynics heaped ridicule on the miracle story, surprised as William Kelly said, that the Mormons so astute in other ways, "can be gulled and gammoned after this fashion."[88] Another, Jerome Howard, "not being myself very superstitious . . . could not be gulled into a belief of the miracle." He saw no gulls but plenty of crickets confined, for some reason, to the uncultivated lands.[89] Nevertheless, the critics were happy to be able to replenish their larders from the harvested grain saved from destructions by the seagulls.

After their first view of the Mormon city with its adobe houses and adjacent fields of ripening cereals, the weary emigrants were anxious to obtain a square meal of green vegetables. The monotonous diet of two to three months of trail food—mostly bread, bacon and coffee—had built up a longing for fresh garden produce. Some experienced travelers recognized this as an early warning of scurvy, the third most common debilitating disease on the overland after cholera and mountain fever.[90] The sight of Mormon gardens brought visions of green peas, beans, and corn according to one famished adventurer.[91]

Perhaps remembering their own hunger for greens during the Pioneer trek, many Saints invited emigrants to dine with them. Charles Ferguson recorded, "They invariably asked us to eat, and would hardly take no for an answer."[92] McDiarmid overcame his negative perception of the Saints long enough to sit down to a table "loaded with good things which we eat with an eager skill. . . ."[93] while Abram Sortore's party was invited into the homes of sixteen of Brigham Young's wives who gave the gold seekers all the vegetables they wanted and treated them nicely.[94] Those not welcomed in were usually furnished meals at fifty cents a customer.[95] Some emigrants were more than willing to pick "peas and other truck on shares" or to "pod peas" so they could get a few meals.[96] When a housewife explained that she could not furnish sleeping accommodations, Dow Stephens did not complain as long as he could be granted vegetables. "Never before or since have I asked anything that was so good, and we ate and ate until we could eat no more, and only felt sorry that our capacity was so limited." He thought the fifty-cent meal was worth five dollars at least. Another traveler commented, "I also had *fresh fish, pot cheese, butter, green peas, rye bread & milk & buckwheat cakes*, which to an appetite of 75 *days continuance* seemed perfectly delicious."[97]

The craving for garden vegetables was so intense that the travelers lived almost exclusively on them while stopped at Salt Lake "at the risk of a fit of sickness," as James Hutchings expressed it.[98] One company did suffer from luxuriating on so many "dainties" that a few of their members became ill with "Mormon fever" as William Johnston called their irresistible malady.[99] Sitting on chairs at a table with all the comforts of home around them only added to the Thanksgiving banquet atmosphere of overindulgence. William Black was reverently impressed with a simple meal of milk, pigweed greens, and bread. His "uncultured Mormon" host offered a blessing on the food, the first such prayer Black had ever heard in his life![100]

Many of the overlanders chose to cook their own meals or were forced to do so. They were able to purchase cheese, butter, and milk. The milk sold for twenty cents "a pale,"[101] while cheese went for twelve cents a pound.[102] Butter, at fifty cents a pound, was not plentiful and bread was also scarce but could be purchased in very limited quantities.[103] Andrew Jackson Allen sold some homemade bread to a group of emigrants who were "nearly starved for bread. My wife had just baked a loaf and have it they must. . . ." He accepted some dried fruit in exchange.[104] As for liquor, the easterners soon found that most of their Mormon hosts did not use intoxicating drinks. Langworthy was sure it was from necessity rather than choice.[105]

Of all the common garden vegetables, only potatoes were in short supply.[106] Late-arriving emigrants found an extra delicacy in the abundance of watermelons—Hutchings reported an alliterative after-supper snack of "mush, milk and melons."[107] A member of Riley Senter's party was able to procure a number of free melons for his group by passing himself off as a "brother" in the local church.[108]

While many gold tourists camped out, probably just as many boarded with Mormon families in order, as Charles Gray explained, *"to set at a table where things were cooked by a woman & everything appearing so nice & clean put us all in excellent spirits."*[109] Arrangements were informal. Most sought out likely-looking homes and often shifted to other abodes if they thought the accommodations were better. The grateful emigrants seemed uniformly well-satisfied with the hospitality and "civility" which they received from their Mormon hosts.[110] The meals were good; the beds were soft; and the prices were reasonable—usually five dollars a week.[111] Patty Sessions made thirty dollars for waiting on a group of travelers and was so sorry for one that she gave him three dollars.[112] A few destitute pilgrims hired out to shock grain or do carpentry, although they were more interested in the board than in the wages.[113] Others rented or even purchased houses during their sojourn in the city because there were no hotels. In the summer of 1850 a corner of the State House was partitioned off as a public restaurant to accommodate emigrants and laborers on public works, and a few entrepreneurs began to plan for the construction of some large boarding houses for the 1851 season.[114]

Having satisfied themselves with some meals of peas and other garden vegetables, the westward-bound adventurers began planning the last portion of their journey through the desert wastes along the Humboldt River and over the awesome Sierra Nevadas to California. Since leaving the Missouri River as well-organized companies under rather grandiloquent titles and with carefully fashioned constitutions and bylaws, they had learned that the only unifying force was their greed for gold, which could easily be shattered by any ill wind blowing along the Platte and Mormon trails. Impatient emigrants, annoyed by slow-moving partners, took off on their own until "all were finally sorted out by speed," according to Edward W. McIlhany.[115] Large trains broke up quite rapidly as their members discovered the difficulty of finding enough grass for all the draft animals and personal animosities increased under the rigors and disappointments of travel. These accumulating irritations finally resulted in many emigrants proceeding on their own or attaching themselves to other groups more in tune with their trail habits. Companies that did manage to stay together often reached a parting of the ways at Salt Lake City where dissolution reigned supreme.

Many of the gold-hungry nomads, realizing that the most difficult portion of the journey lay ahead, decided to abandon their wagons at Salt Lake to pack through before winter storms trapped them in the Sierras. Some listened to rumors that wagons had never yet crossed the California ranges and that it was impossible to do so. As Charles Gould wrote, "We have decided to leave our wagons and pack our animals in order to facilitate our progress in the remaining part of our journey...."[116] Great numbers of diaries and journals emphasized this decision to reoutfit in Salt Lake City for the last dash to the diggings.[117]

Reasons for split-ups of companies ranged from members who were ill who stayed in Salt Lake City to emigrants who just wanted a rest before tackling the desert. The impatient ones left after only a day or so; some of the fainthearted decided to winter in the valley. Other groups differed over which of three main trails to take—Hastings Cutoff, the Salt Lake Road, or the Old Spanish Trail to Los Angeles.[118] The Ithaca and California Mining Company was typical of a company that dissolved because of differences over the departure time from Salt Lake.[119]

Another adventurer, Jackson Thomason, regretted the breach of faith committed by his company members in abandoning their sick in the Mormon city and was especially perturbed because he was forced to divide the property on Sunday and missed going to church. Thomason was a very religious man and had also insisted on resting every Sabbath while other gold-rushers passed him by. "A compulsive meanderer . . . born with his feet in the road," he had departed Pontostoc County, Mississippi, with the California Exploring and Mining Company to satisfy his everlasting curiosity and only, supplementally, to make his fortune. He had been in the mercantile business and was wholly unsuited to a pioneering venture, but he managed to travel in some comfort across the plains. When some of his party became ill and the company broke up in Salt Lake, he joined another group. Eventually Thomason returned to the South from the mines with a gold-headed cane as his only financial reward.[120]

Many of the dissolutions were laced with hostility. Occasionally members would buy out a particularly obnoxious partner's interest just to get rid of him.[121] Even with the best of intentions the division of a company left "much difficulty & dissatisfaction . . . after a few days consideration."[122] Some groups found it impossible to reach an amicable disposition of their property and ended up in a Salt Lake City court before a Mormon judge, a much larger problem that is discussed in a later chapter on the legal problems between Saint and Gentile.[123]

With gold mining companies splitting up and packing through to California, a very active trading market opened up in Salt Lake City. The purchase and sale of goods by emigrants and Saints alike was based mostly on barter rather than cash, even though the Mormon leadership had established a coinage system backed by gold dust brought from California by returning members of the Mormon Battalion. One eastern adventurer, arriving late in 1849, reported that the ex-soldiers had brought as much as $300,000 in gold with them and that he had accidentally seen a single bag which contained sixty pounds of dust.[124] This was an exaggeration, but there was enough for paper currency to be issued and for $2.50, $5.00, $10.00, and $20.00 gold pieces to be minted. The coinage started in September 1849 and continued until early 1851 when Brigham Young ended the experiment because the supply of gold had dwindled and, more importantly, because the relative fineness of the metal was not up to par and resulted in a discounting of the coins outside the limits of Mormondom by as much as twenty-five percent.[125] Californians especially denounced the overvalued gold pieces as being "debased," "spurious," and "vile falsehoods," but to the Saints in Salt Lake Valley the $75,000 worth of gold coins furnished a plentiful supply of money for commercial purposes during the two years in which the pieces circulated.[126]

Until the influx of emigrants the Mormon people had considered money to be of little value and preferred to trade scarce goods for eastern articles they wanted, usually refusing to accept any money at all. On the other hand, they were quite willing to pay in gold dust or coins for desired merchandise from the newcomers.[127] One Mormon, Zerah Pulsipher, refused to sell some cornmeal to an emigrant for five dollars in coin when so many poor were starving[128] while Josselyn wrote his wife in Ohio, "We can trade groceries for anything that they have, but they will not sell for money for they have plenty and cannot buy what they want with it."[129] The abundant evidence from overland diaries seems to contradict a charge made later against the Mormons by Nelson Slater in a denunciatory pamphlet. He claimed that the Saints deliberately withheld cash from the emigrants to avoid draining money from the Great Basin. Slater, a schoolteacher from New York who had his wife and three children with him, decided to winter in Salt Lake Valley before continuing his journey to California. Smarting from perceived discrimination at the hands of his Mormon hosts, he collaborated with Philip L. Pratt in 1852 to publish at Coloma, California, a ninety-four-page condemnation of the Mormon people and their leaders entitled *Fruits of Mormonism; Or, A Fair and Candid Statement of Facts Illustrative of Mormon Principles, Mormon Policy, and Mormon Character, by More than Forty Eyewitnesses.* The pamphlet became welcome evidence for writers and editors all over the nation to substantiate their anti-Mormon charges and suspicions.[130]

The rush for gold and the passage of eager excursionists through the Mormon Zion brought denunciations from Brigham Young that the hunger for gold would destroy men's souls and might bring ruin to the United States. He thought that the nation now had "a puke" in California gold which would prove to be a curse rather than a blessing. He said of the emigrants, "Our city has been filled with lawyers, doctors, priests, merchants, mechanics, etc. etc., who, after cursing

Joseph Smith all their lives as a money digger, are marching half distracted with excitement and gold fever, to quietly lay down their honorable, legal, or sacred professions for the honorable calling of money diggers."[131] Joseph G. Hovey heard one sermon in which his church President prophesied that gold "has overthrode nations and Kingdoms. And . . . that it will be the means of overthrough this nation that has drove us out. . . ."[132]

As for those church members who persisted in wanting to leave Zion for the fleshpots of the American River, Young said, "if they have a golden god in their hearts, they had better stay where they are."[133] In sermon after sermon, Brigham Young and other leaders pointed out the advantages of remaining in Salt Lake Valley to till the soil instead of rushing off to unhealthy California where young men soon became "rude and uncultivated"[134] and where they would fail to make their fortunes anyway.[135] In one outburst, the Mormon President challenged any would-be adventurer to choose fifty men to go with him to the mines while the Prophet would select only twenty-five farmers to stay and work with him in the valley. Young predicted that at the end of a year the fifty would not be able to buy out the twenty-five while the bones of some of the gold seekers might well "lie bleaching" on the prairie.[136] Joseph L. Robinson copied Young's sentiments by carrying a banner in the Pioneer Day parade proclaiming "Truth Before Gold,"[137] while poet laureate William Clayton composed a six-stanza ode to "The Gold Diggers" for the celebration. It ended with the words.

> Now, ye Saints, my advice I will give without price,
> Don't be tempted to worship the dust;
> But stick close to your farms, and build up your good barns,
> For the grain is much better I trust.[138]

As the emigrants listened to these Sunday homilies, they believed the admonitions were just further proof that the Mormon leaders had already discovered rich gold deposits in the nearby mountains and were only waiting for the argonauts' departure before directing Mormon miners to the new fields.[139] A correspondent for the *New York Herald* wrote his paper that if there was gold on the western side of the Sierra Nevada it was only logical there would also be gold on the eastern slopes which were in Mormon territory.[140] Many emigrants agreed with him. Alonzo C. Clay wrote that after he and his party had exploited the California district for gold, they would stop at Salt Lake City on their return journey to the states " and refil our bags for you know that it is rather slippery and we may lose some of it."[141] Dow Stephens and his partners sneaked out of the city at 10 o'clock one night to travel up Little Cottonwood Canyon where they spent five or six fruitless days searching for a gold mine.[142] A few agreed with D. A. Millington that there was probably no gold east of the Sierras and that anyway the Mormons were afraid that if gold were found in the Great Basin it would ruin them when they left their farms looking for the elusive metal.[143]

But there was no hesitation on the part of the Mormon hierarchy to collect tithing on the riches being hauled out of the earth by the brethren in California. Almon W. Babbitt, agent for the church in the eastern states, told Goldsborough Bruff that the Salt Lake authorities had collected a barrel of gold dust in tithes by midsummer of 1849.[144] The church secretary recorded a more modest sum of $4,012 received in one mail from Amasa Lyman in California.[145] In their first General Epistle of July 1849, the Mormon presidency reminded the Saints in California that they had "it in their power to do much good" by forwarding their donations to Salt Lake City.[146] And the Prophet himself was not immune to the lure of the precious metal. In a letter of April 5, 1849, to Samuel Brannan, the leading church elder in California, Brigham Young asked Brannan to pay his tithing, a sum estimated at $10,000, and added that Brother Brigham would appreciate a gift of $20,000 to help him in his labors. Then, not forgetting his faithful counselors, he asked the supposedly wealthy Brannan to send an additional sum of $20,000 to be divided between Heber C. Kimball and Willard Richards "who, like myself, are straitened." There is no record that Elder Brannan ever responded.[147]

Brigham Young directed his followers along two paths— a public policy of discouraging members from going to California because of a feared mass exodus from the valley and a private agenda of dispatching "gold missions" to bring needed capital into Zion. In the Third General Epistle of the church, the President very carefully delineated between those who were sent *"by counsel"* and those who went by the "counsel of their own wills and covetous feelings. . . . Let such leave their carcasses where they do their work, we want not our burial grounds polluted with such hypocrites. . . ."[148] In the fall of 1849, Young sent one company of about twenty young men to work the mines under the direction of Apostles Charles C. Rich and Amasa Lyman and another group of about thirty under the leadership of Simpson D. Huffaker.[149] In addition, the Prophet advised church leaders of the Council of Fifty to grubstake two or more persons each in a search for gold "for their own advantage . . . owing to the large amount of time spent by them in counciling for the public. . . ." While the gold missions were able to bring into Utah at least $80,000 in gold, most of the individual partnerships were as unsuccessful as "Brother Thurber [who] worked a year, made nothing, and came home glad for the clothes he had left with us."[150] Emigrant suspicions were correct about the Mormon leadership being more interested in acquiring California gold than their Sunday fulminations from the pulpit against gold seeking might indicate. As soon as Brigham Young was assured that the Mormon colony was firmly established in the Great Basin, he felt secure enough to risk some private gold ventures.

Safely ensconced in their mountain home lying between what Major Stephen H. Long had labeled, in 1820, the "Great American Desert" and the even worse expanse of aridity soon to be known as Nevada, the Mormon people were astounded when the deluge of gold-hungry emigrants descended on them in June of 1849. But they were not as amazed as were these eager travelers who, used to the green verdure of the eastern seaboard and the Ohio and Mississippi valleys and exhausted by their dusty trip across the plains, all at once were greeted by the sight of homes and gardens and green fields in a settled habitation at the Great Salt Lake oasis. From this time until the western migration after the Civil War began to fill the Great Plains with towns and farms, the Mormon settlement served as the chief way station for rest and recruitment for pioneers on their way to the Pacific Coast.

Most of the forty-niners had difficulty understanding why the Saints were not also en route to the gold fields of the Sierra Nevada along with the rest of mankind, but were quick to accept the hospitality of their hosts whose garden vegetables and soft beds were a welcome respite from the rigors of the trail. Many of the argonauts were well-educated and cultured people from eastern cities and as far away as England, as attested by their descriptive and well-written journals.

Although these mostly male-dominated parties were interested in only a brief stopover in Salt Lake Valley to prepare for the last dash across the western deserts of the Great Basin, their diaries have left a fascinating picture of the Mormon settlement.

The gold rush made a dramatic change in the lifestyles of Brigham Young and his followers and broke the isolation they had sought from persecution and harassment. Emigrant letters to relatives and newspapers back home and soon-to-be published diaries carried news of the Mormons and reintroduced them to the reading public of the east. Instead of being left to enjoy anonymity in their Wasatch Mountain villages, the Mormon people were again projected onto the national stage where, soon, a new political party would declare that the twin relics of barbarism—slavery and polygamy—must be abolished.

chapter four

GREAT BASIN OPEN AIR MARKET

M ANY pilgrims arrived in Salt Lake City in 1849 "almost famishing with fatigue and want of food"[1] and "nearly destitute of provisions."[2] With starvation facing them, they were relieved and heartened by the advantages the Mormon settlement offered.[3] Not only were their food supplies exhausted, but their mules and oxen were jaded or given out. Forced driving of stock over ruinous roads damaged draft animals, and this was the most serious obstacle to continuing the trip to California.[4] John B. Chamberlain noted, "The fatigue of drawing the wagon has nearly killed the mules, so that we will have to lie here some time to recruit."[5] The animals of one outfit were in such bad shape that the travelers spent six weeks attempting to resuscitate the stock.[6]

Most travelers stayed about a week, as did Jackson Thomason. He recorded, "Our oxen all look much better [and] the few days rest they have taken here in good grass has recruited them considerable. The grass here is inexhaustible & the stock belonging to the Mormons are just as fat as they can roll in their skin."[7] The excellent pasturage in the valley gave the pioneer settlers an unrivaled opportunity to pick up exhausted animals and to see the stock rejuvenated in a short time and ready for sale or trade to other needy emigrants.[8] While the overlanders recruited and rested themselves as well as their stock, being "very much fatigued and enervated" after their journey,[9] they also took the opportunity to repair their wagons and equipment and to get their animals shod—or had "some shouse made" as William Wilson quaintly stated.[10]

The argonauts of 1850 faced even grimmer conditions on the trail. They thought they had learned something from the overly-burdened wayfarers of the previous year and so lightened their wagons of provisions hoping to get fresh supplies at the forts along the way or, surely, at Salt Lake City. Secondly, drier conditions resulted in a scantier supply of grass. They ended up feeding their stock from dwindling supplies of provisions.[11] Brigham Young warned, in a sermon printed in the *Deseret News* on July 20, 1850, that travelers should not depend on the Saints for bread and supplies. "We had to divide the bread which we had for our own families last year with them to keep them alive; and we shall have to do the same this year." He added that he hoped in another year or two his people would be able to help emigrants with food so that they would "not be disappointed as many are, this season." In the same sermon he chastised his followers: "You have no right to sell your flour to emigrants, to feed horses and mules, and rob this people of their bread." But he also voiced another concern: "When a stranger comes here, tell him where his teams may recruit, and if you will not give the strangers good counsel, you are not fit for good society."

In June, before the harvest, early arrivals found it impossible to buy even an ounce of flour.[12] Two men from one company spent an entire day going from house to house in the city gathering forty pounds of cornmeal and a similar amount of "shorts" a residue from milling that included the germ, fine bran, and some flour. They mixed them together before continuing their journey to California.[13] The Mormon church manuscript history noted in July that "our flour mills, five in number, are all crowded, grinding for the immigrants, who are hanging round in hungry hordes, begging for enough to feed them to the gold mines. . . ."[14] Gentiles and Saints had to share the grain harvest of 1850.

Many of the emigrants, particularly in the second year of the rush to California, ran out of money as well as provisions by the time they reached the Mormon metropolis and found it necessary to hire out to their hosts to finance the rest of the trip. A few of the adventurers were fortunate enough to find professional jobs in teaching or medicine; most were forced into some form of manual labor including harvesting, haying, carpentry, blacksmithing, shoemaking, tailoring, fetching firewood from the canyons, digging irrigation ditches, fencing, making shingles, or cutting timber for the sawmills—backbreaking occupations to which many of them were not accustomed.[15] One enterprising Salt Lake owner of a blacksmith shop advertised in the *Deseret News* on July 1, 1850, that emigrants could get work helping to construct the Golden Pass Road and receive "an *honorable compensation*" while his crew shod their animals and repaired their wagons.

The majority of travelers accepted the modest sum of $2.25 plus board for several days work or flour in exchange for helping to cut, shock, and thresh grain.[16] At the height of the harvest there were not enough emigrants to go around, and Brigham Young found it necessary to spend part of a sermon in an entreaty for assistance—"Friends, help us to gather our harvest, and then you shall have what you want, and you can then go and gather riches."[17] Langworthy was one who responded, but he also gave a scientific lecture in the Bowery to raise funds for his trip.[18] One Saint, Joseph Hovey, expressed his gratitude for the aid from outsiders. "The Lorde has truly open up the way before us . . . in halping or causing the goldigers coming this way and being oblige to stop here to get a fitout to the mines   if it had not bin for the gold digers we would not be able to harvest our grain. . . ."[19] Patty Sessions was more succinct about her struggle to clean her yard of weeds—"Got our emigrant to hoe it."[20]

During the harrowing period of starvation in the late winter of 1848–49, Heber C. Kimball, second-in-command to Young, had uttered a defiant prophesy. Many references to it appear in autobiographies and reminiscences. Joseph Harker merely noted in his "Journal," "at conferance [April 1849] H. C. Kimble Profiside that we should have clothing in Salt Lake City as cheepe as it was in New York City. . . ."[21] George Morris' description in his "Autobiography" added, "As soon as he uttered it he said he felt scared almost out of his wits to think that he had predicted such an unlikely thing as that. Brother George A. Smith who was sitting right by him spoke to him and said, 'There, Brother Kimball, you have burst your boiler this time sure.' "[22] Kimball's own remembrance of the incident fourteen years later was that he had said, " 'Never mind, boys, in less than one year there will be plenty of clothes and everything that we shall want sold at less than St. Louis prices;' and I thought when I came to reflect upon it that it was a very improbable thing." Kimball added, "Brother [Charles C.] Rich told me that he thought I had done up the job at prophesying that time, but the sequel showed the prediction to be of the Lord."[23]

By spring of 1849 the Saints were almost destitute—clothing was worn out, their farm implements were "getting used up, broken, or destroyed," and their wagons were in disrepair because of lack of iron to fix them.[24] At this very critical stage in founding a Mormon refuge in the Rockies, "the Gentiles came powering in from Different parts of the Earth on their way for the Mines" and left with their hosts in Salt Lake City, through barter or by exchange of cash, "Horses Oxen Waggons Cloathing Ploughs Spades Shovels Hoes Saws Augers Chisels Plains. . . . This Caused the Saints to wax fat so that all Seamed to have a plenty of money and means to make them comfortable. . . ."[25] Joseph Holbrook thought that "it literally seemed that the Lord inspired them to load down their wagons with everything that the saints need for tools, to wear as clothes, for food. . . ."[26] Andrew Allen wrote that "many [of the] things thay did not kneed . . . they soald . . . to us verry cheap. . . ."[27] Joseph Hovey was grateful: "Truly do I rejoice in my God for his goodness for just as we are all most out of bread they have come and oblige to sell there flower and there Bake and a little of all their provisions an Clothing   it is in the right time for we as a people are very destitytute. . . ."[28] Adventurers from the East began furnishing local citizens with the supplies the Saints had been unable to bring with them during the hurried exodus from Illinois and which had been unobtainable for two years. Mormon pioneer journals overflow with expressions of thanksgiving for the mercantile harvests of the summers of 1849 and 1850.[29]

Individual emigrants were not alone in dumping their possessions in the Mormon capital. Large companies were formed for the express purpose of transporting wholesale goods of every description to California gold-diggers to garner huge profits. These were forced to join in selling or trading their goods at Salt Lake City. Mormon Bishop Benjamin Brown described the result: "These persons procured just the things they would have done had they been forming companies purposely for relieving the Saints, and had they determined to do it as handsomely as unlimited wealth would allow."[30] Unable to retrace their journey back to the States and half crazy to get to the gold fields, the entrepreneurs sold or bartered their articles for whatever they could get.[31] Salt Lake Valley became a place of general deposit for all kinds of goods and "thus began the riches of the Gentiles to flow to us . . . ," as enthusiastic Charles Lambert expressed it.[32]

Benjamin Johnson has left a poignant description of the trans-
formation that occurred when the gold adventurers entered the Salt
Lake Valley in 1849:

> Sunday, the 15th of June came. It was a beautiful day, but noth-
> ing looked beautiful to me. The very heavens seemed brass over
> our heads. I did not wish to go to meeting; if I did, I was barefoot,
> and so I wandered out from a home of prospective starvation and
> nakedness. . . . Brother Burnham came to me and I said to him,
> "Jacob, there is one consolation to us left. If we starve, The Lord
> certainly will give us credit for industry if nothing else. We have
> worked hard in hunger and weakness, but it does almost seem now
> that he has forgotten us?" As we were talking we saw some boys
> coming upon the run, who said a company of emigrants had just
> come in from the States. I said it could not be so, for it seemed
> impossible for a company to get through by the 15th of June. . . .
> [I] soon found it true, for a company *was* there; and almost their
> first inquiry was for pack saddles, and fresh animals in place of their
> *jaded* ones. They appeared almost crazy with excitement about
> California and gold. I traded them a jack and jenny and began the
> making of pack saddles, rigging them with rawhide. And oh! what
> a change! I now could get flour, bacon, sugar, rice, soap, tea powder,
> lead, tobacco, the finest clothing, with Wagons, harness, etc. etc. in
> exchange for a packing outfits, which I could supply in quantity.[33]

The manufacture of packsaddles became a profitable business for other
valley residents who joined in the homemade gold rush. Jonathan
Crosby converted his furniture shop into a saddlery and accepted
wagons, groceries, and clothing in return for leather goods.[34] Other
Saints worked out in the open to provide the accouterments for pack
animals.[35]

Hammering out trades for lighter pack horses and mules drove
some emigrants to desperate measures. Mormon residents were reluctant to part with their animals and would finally only accept generous
offers. Joseph Hovey noted that a Saint could get a good wagon and
two sets of harness for a horse and "most any kind at that and sometimes 5 times as much as a horse is worth. . . ."[36] The demand was so
great that "the brethren got many very good trades which ware a great
blessing," according to Andrew Allen.[37]

George Morris, who "never was one to trade," lost two small
three-year-old steers during the winter. After a long search, he found
them fat and in good condition. He put them under yoke and headed

for home. As he passed a camp of gold diggers, one of them offered to trade a large yoke of footsore oxen for Morris' small team. Morris demurred saying he needed his for hauling firewood. After haggling, Morris finally accepted the two large oxen, a third ox, and ten dollars in trade for his runty animals. He then turned his three newly-acquired oxen loose to run in the "mire bottoms" for four days. This cured their sore feet so that "no one could tell from their looks that they had crossed the plains that season." Returning with his refreshed animals he was stopped by another group of emigrants who wanted to trade for them "without asking me a single question about whether they had crossed the plains that summer or not the cattle looked so well and walked off so spry and lively that they did not even suspect that they had." In this second trade he received two yoke of oxen, fifteen dollars, and a wagon that had cost the owner $110. He engaged in other bargaining, and by the end of the tourist season he had acquired five yoke of oxen, a wagon, and four cows plus clothing, boots, shoes, bread, and groceries "sufficient to make us more comfortable than we had ever been before," all for the two scrubby animals that had started him on his shopping venture.[38]

In trading for animals, not many pioneers did as well as George Morris. Chapman Duncan, however, started his bargaining with one yoke of oxen and by fall had two yoke of oxen, two colts, two mules, and one horse.[39] Zadok Judd did almost as well for two horses. He received three yoke of cattle, a good wagon, a cook stove, a dozen shirts, a silver watch, some tools, and a half barrel of pork.[40] The usual trade was two worn-out yoke of oxen for one fresh yoke and two jaded horses for one fresh one.[41] Milch cows were exchanged by both pilgrim and valley resident with one pilgrim obtaining "to good cows which I kneeded verry much. . . ."[42]

Wagons became so plentiful in Salt Lake City that Mormon leaders stopped buying any to use to bring in new converts from the Missouri River.[43] As Joseph Robinson wrote, in good biblical phraseology, "Yea we got from them some provisions and a great deal of clothing tools good horses footsore and poor cattle and waggons. . . ."[44] Benjamin Johnson acquired so many wagons that he stripped them of their iron and burned the wood for fuel.

In one incident an emigrant came to Johnson's home late on a Saturday night wanting to buy some packsaddles, insisting that his company was leaving the next morning and that he could not wait until Monday for Johnson to make some. So the tradesman got up early Sunday and worked until meeting time. The overlander gave Johnson three sets of harness and a new wagon "with more camp outfit, clothing and goods in [it] than a fair price to pay four fold for my work. When they got what they wanted they cared for nothing they had to leave."[45] Brigham Young thought such transactions to be a "mutual blessing."[46]

While the overlanders sought out packsaddles and fresh stock from among the Mormons, the Saints were eagerly trading for goods they craved. They made frequent visits to the camps and wagons.[47] When Patty Sessions found she could get nothing she wanted at the tiny local store, she "went to some wagons" where she was able to buy a pair of shoes and other manufactured articles.[48] William Kelly noted that the Mormons expected to be able to supply "their little wants" from emigrant wagons.[49]

Some of the wants were not so little. Dow Stephens wrote that many of the Mormon women were barefooted and scantily dressed and that their clothing was practically worn out after two years of privation and separation from any source of supply.[50] Emigrant Beeson Townsend observed that next to sugar and coffee the articles most in demand at the wagon-box stores were calicoes and ladies' shoes.[51] Many of these clothing necessities were supplied by the travelers, causing William Leany to note with irony that clothing was now being supplied "by the hands of many who ware the means of our Expulsion from the States. . . ."[52] The fine apparel that easterners brought with them to wear in California was traded off for a mere trifle[53] or even given away. One traveler presented his host, Mosiah L. Hancock, with a new brown broadcloth suit as an expression of respect because the Saint had taken the time to explain Mormon theology to the company.[54] John Udell was in such a hurry to get to the gold fields that he and his party put what goods they could on their horses, sold their wagons, and threw away much of their clothing.[55]

Groceries were in great demand and the coming of the gold seekers made them available.[56] William Johnston was confident that there were more groceries in any one wagon of his train than in all Salt Lake City, with the possible exception of the "harems" of Brigham Young.[57] The Mormon people were not willing to sell anything but would immediately trade for provisions of any kind: flour, bacon, sugar, dried fruit, spices, rice, and especially tea and coffee. For every diary account that mentioned other foods desired there were at least a half dozen that listed coffee and tea as being the most wanted of all emigrant products—sugar, of course, was usually a part of the request.[58] One traveler explained how the Saints had been "weaned from the luxuries of civilization, unless we except tea and coffee, which the women were extremely anxious to obtain from us."[59] In fact, they would give almost any price to obtain them.[60] Coffee sold for fifty cents a pound.[61] Mosiah Hancock was the recipient of a gift of one hundred pounds of the bean, which he carefully noted in his autobiography was later traded off.[62] William Johnston reported, "One lady begged a handful of coffee, saying that in two years she had not tasted that beverage. Another asked for as much as would make a cupful for a sick friend."[63]

Tea was in even greater demand. James Hutchings made a profit of one hundred percent by selling tea at three dollars a pound after he had paid only a dollar and a half for it.[64] G. W. Thissell was sure he could get a cartload of eggs for a pound of tea, and most travelers soon discovered that they could obtain fresh vegetables by trading tea.[65] Dow Stephens wrote that his wagon had barely come to a stop in the city when "we were soon surrounded by the Mormons, principally women inquiring for tea, and if we had any to sell. They seemed to be as much starved for tea as we were for vegetables. . . . Some of the women said they had not tasted tea for two years past."[66]

Flour was also important. Benjamin Ashby was grateful to a party of adventurers who gave him a peck of broken crackers which his family used to thicken their rations of milk. He later worked all day making a pair of shoes for a pint of shorts, which his mother shared with a neighbor who had eaten nothing but greens for several weeks.[67] Aroet Hale was invited to eat a meal by the first group of emigrants he met—"the best supper I ever ate"—after which they gave him ten pounds of flour and ten pounds of bacon. His sister "wept for joy" and immediately baked some white bread which they had not tasted for months.[68]

There were special luxuries some Saints hungered for—liquor and tobacco.[69] The lack of any tavern in the settlement was soon challenged by emigrant wagons dispensing "Alkihaul" at four dollars a gallon.[70] The editor of the Mormon *Frontier Guardian*, on September 5, 1849, wrote of the introduction of liquor to the Saints. "When the alcohol was brought forward and sold, it threw some of them off their legs. . . . They were not wise to hazard a contest with so potent an enemy, more to be dreaded than the mobs of Illinois." James Philly had little difficulty in selling the remainder of his stock of tobacco in Salt Lake City for five dollars a pound, although he had been able to get only one dollar a pound on the trail.[71] William Kelly took pity on several local citizens and "gave them some tobacco, of which they said they were in great need."[72]

Other goods disposed of in Salt Lake City by the overburdened emigrants included tools, copper kettles, and all types of cutlery and hardware.[73] When James Kleiser's wagon overturned crossing Weber River, dumping a dozen Ames shovels into the stream, a local farmer offered to pay the owner the price of the shovels as listed in St. Louis for the dubious possibility of recovering them.[74] Priddy Meeks bought a scythe for three bits which the seller said was too soft and of no account. Meeks tempered it by soaking it for several days in cold spring water and it turned out to be the sweetest scythe he had ever used.[75] Other Saints traded for whole libraries of books. Benjamin Johnson accumulated a number of physicians' libraries plus enough drugs to establish a small pharmacy.[76] The ladies were not left out. They traded for needles and thread and such refinements as beads and perfumed soaps.[77]

Prices for equipment and stock reflected the bargain-basement atmosphere surrounding the bartering and cash exchanges. Wagons selling in the states for as much as $125.00 now went for from $5.50 to $25.00.[78] William Lorton parted with his $180 wagon for $25.[79] In another trade, four heavy wagons plus a yoke of oxen were offered for one light Yankee wagon.[80] Carriages worth $150 often sold for $30.[81] A set of harness costing from $30 to $50 now sold for between $2 and $15.[82] Mormon pioneers did very well; one Saint, Charles Lambert, reflected that "great bargains was got at times. . . ."[83]

Emigrants were willing to pay the price for faster horses and mules instead of slow-plodding oxen. Valley prices for light stock rose from $25 to $30 in the spring to $100, then to $150, and finally to $200.[84] "Mules . . . can't be had at that," according to Thomas D. Scroggins.[85] The price of oxen fell until they became "a drug."[86]

While seasonal prices skyrocketed in the Salt Lake Valley, it must be remembered that at the Missouri River towns of Independence and St. Joseph the cost of a choice mule at outfitting time could be as much as $125; the price of a yoke of oxen varied from $45 to $60.[87] The booming market at the City of the Saints encouraged Dimmick Huntington to contract with Chief Walker of the local Ute tribe to sell horses stolen from California by the Indians to the needy gold-rushers.[88] Despite the burgeoning prices, William Kelly was able to exchange and purchase horses and mules on what he considered "very favourable terms."[89] Perhaps this depended upon how well-heeled you were by the time you reached Salt Lake City. Blacksmithing charges were reasonable. The price for shoeing a horse or mule ranged from $1 per foot,[90] the usual cost, to the "moderate price of seven dollars" exacted by one lady blacksmith. Oxen could be shod for from $8 to $10.[91]

Prices for flour in 1849 started out at $2 per 100 pounds in early March, rose to $5 by late May, to $10 by early July, then to $15, and finally to $25 before the new harvest lowered the price to $10 by the first of September. But this fluctuation was mild compared to prices faced by emigrants in 1850. Flour rose to $50 per 100 pounds on June 19, to $100 on June 25, and then only for small quantities. At this point, Brigham Young, in a special message to his missionaries abroad, expostulated that the chimera of a handsome profit induced "some of our speculators to sell their last morsel and go without." The beginning of the harvest in early July dropped the price to $25 where it remained until mid-August when it gradually declined to $10 per 100 pounds by November. The price of wheat followed the same curve. It rose from $5 a bushel for "frostbitten" wheat in the early spring of 1849 to $10 by mid-July and then back down to as low as $3 by October. The 1850 prices went from $4 per bushel, up to $8 in July, and back to $4 again by November.[92] The Mormon leader had proposed on July 8, 1849, the establishment of an arbitrary price of $5 per bushel for wheat,[93] but the law of supply and demand defeated the noble effort. The prices for wheat and flour were just as high at other stops along the Overland Trail during the gold rush years. The cost of flour was only about $6 at its peak in 1851 and fell to $3 in 1852.[94]

Except for sugar, coffee, bacon, dried fruits, and tea, other groceries sold from fifty to seventy-five percent below wholesale prices in the states. Sugar averaged about $.50 per pound in 1849 and $.75 the next year; coffee followed a similar pattern although at one point the 1850 price rose to $1.50 a pound; bacon remained near $.12 a pound in 1849 and could not be obtained at all the next year at $.75; dried fruits reached $1.00 a pound in 1850; and tea hovered between $3.00 and $4.00 a pound during both years. Dairy products were more reasonable: butter was $.20 a pound in 1849 and about $.50 in 1850; cheese went from $.15 to about $.30; and milk sold for $.10 a quart both years. Of other common products, rice rose from $.25 a pound to $.35 cents in 1850; potatoes sold for from $1.00 to $4.00 a bushel in 1850; eggs could not "be had at any price; they are all wanted for setting purposes," according to McKeeby; beef was about $.10 a pound in 1849 and varied from "plenty" at $.07 to $.75 in 1850; chickens were $.50 apiece. By the second year of overland travel, an emigrant could buy a pie in Salt Lake City for $.50. Among dry goods, calico sold for $.35 a yard in 1849 and $.40 in 1850. Vests, which seemed to be a very necessary part of male attire at the time, sold for $1.50 each in St. Louis but could be bought for 3 bits or for about $.37 in Salt Lake. Moccasins were $1.00 a pair; a piece of sole leather was $.60; sheeting went for about $.08 a yard; glass was $16.00 for a half box; shovels were $.50 each. A set of joiner's tools which sold for $150 in St. Louis could be bought for $25 in the valley; wood was $10 per cord; and lumber was $5 per 100 board feet. Because of the scarcity of firewood, Finley McDiarmid's group had to pay $.25 for a pole to get a fire. There were cries from a few outraged emigrants, but prices for the above items were cheaper at Salt Lake City than at the trading posts along the Overland Trail. Wages, with board, fluctuated from $2.50 to $5.00 a day despite Brigham Young's pious hope that they should remain at a stable $5.00 rate.[95]

The residents of Salt Lake Valley used most of the cash they accumulated from trading with emigrants to purchase supplies from Gentile merchants who had established pioneer stores in the city. In the early gold rush of 1849 a *New York Tribune* reporter noted, "No hotel, sign-post, cake and beer shop, barber pole, market-house, grocery, provision, dry goods, or hardware store distinguished one part of the town from another. . . ."[96] As mentioned earlier, the first stores were wagon-box affairs from which profit-minded adventurers attempted to unload their California goods so they could travel on unencumbered. Most of these itinerant storekeepers had with them from two to ten thousand dollars worth of goods.[97] The two Pomeroy brothers composed a firm with larger vision. They entered Salt Lake in 1849 with thirty tons of merchandise valued at fifty thousand dollars transported by a hundred wagons, each drawn by three or four pair of oxen.[98] Before being allowed to sell out, one Pomeroy was subjected to a trial by Mormon authorities for having taken part in the mob violence in Missouri against the Saints and for having confiscated some of their property. The verdict handed down was that Pomeroy had actually tried to help the Mormons in Missouri and so was "honerably aquited" and allowed to sell his goods.[99]

Perhaps the first established merchant to trade at Salt Lake was Louis Vasquez, partner of Jim Bridger, who sold a small allotment of goods in the city in November 1849.[100] Of much greater importance was the firm of James M. Livingston and John H. Kinkead. They competed for the Mormon trade until 1858 and had such friendly relations with church leaders that they were often invited to special receptions given by Brigham Young.[101] Livingston and Kinkead sold twenty thousand dollars worth of merchandise in the late fall of 1849 within two weeks. Eight or ten clerks were kept busy with people thrusting their money in through the windows.[102] John Taylor thought the ladies were bees and the stores hives—"though unlike in one respect, for the bee goes in full, and comes out empty; but in this case it was reversed." The citizens demanded "goods! Goods! GOODS!,"[103] and the sole restraint on Livingston was to charge only as much as his conscience would allow.[104] John and Enoch Reese were the only Mormon merchants in the early years but their business never reached Livingston and Kinkead's volume. With these merchant companies selling out in a hurry by late November, one emigrant wondered where the Mormon residents would get additional supplies, pinched as they were for necessities.[105]

While Vasquez apparently did not return to the valley in 1850, Livingston and Kinkead, and the Reese Brothers came in with even larger stocks of goods. They were joined by three other firms. Thomas S. Williams built a 75-by-23-foot storehouse just west of the State House and Elijah Thomas opened a store in the 15th Ward House.

More important was the company started by Benjamin Holladay and Theodore F. Warner.[106] They had accumulated some liquid capital by buying and selling, at a good profit, $70,000 worth of Mexican War surplus oxen and equipment. Holladay and Warner sold $150,-000 worth of goods in Salt Lake City in 1850.[107] While the merchant houses endured crowded times, some valley residents grumbled that they were "deceived by the merchants about the quality of groceries" and that there was not a sufficient supply. At Sunday meetings, sermons were delivered denouncing the high prices charged by store owners.[108] Later, Mormon critic Nelson Slater charged that to overcome such opposition some of the merchants joined the Latter-day Saints church.[109] All five companies used the columns of the new church newspaper, the *Deseret News*, to advertise their wares.[110] Two years later the firms were still in business and selling goods at enormous profits, according to overlander Addison Crane.[111]

Local small businessmen also advertised in the *Deseret News* offering individualized services to passing emigrants. There were two informal meat markets, two blacksmiths, three surgeon dentists (one of whom claimed "scurvy effectually cured"), and the proprietor of a homemade eating house.[112] If your watch was losing time, McVicar & Barlow would make the necessary repairs.[113] By 1850 some efforts were being advanced by the local leaders to make the Saints self-sufficient. A pottery works had opened and construction had begun on a small woolen factory and some cutlery establishments.[114] There were five grist mills and eight or nine sawmills in operation.[115] An announcement in the *Deseret News* on September 7, 1850, noted that the foundation for a City Brewery had just been laid. The editor urged hops growers to gather them so that the local people could "resume their pleasure parties."

The news began to travel back to the Missouri River outfitting towns that the Mormon city provided a convenient stopping place for rest and recruitment, and many travelers began to choose this route over the traditional road by way of Fort Hall. Having a crossroads shopping place in the midst of the Great American Desert may well have encouraged more people to brave the terrors of the trail. Established travel patterns changed and thousands of gentiles were introduced to the Mormon settlers. The economic and social interchange between the two groups tended to ameliorate the attitudes and feelings both had and to provide a congenial marketplace for ideas as well as groceries. The eastern visitors discovered that their hosts were normal human beings after all, despite their strange beliefs, while the Saints more and more began to dismiss from their minds the memories of the persecutions and harassments suffered at the hands of the people of Missouri and Illinois.

The needs of the pioneer settlers and of the emigrants were widely publicized by letters, diaries, and word of mouth all along the Oregon and California trails. This initiated the large-scale transportation of goods and merchandise from the Missouri River towns to the Great Basin. The improved social atmosphere at Salt Lake City, and the obvious economic opportunities, attracted gentile entrepreneurs who established mercantile houses. At first their reception was friendly, but over the next two decades, as the Mormon people began to murmur against gouging and high prices and as Brigham Young endeavored to make his people economically self-sufficient, the Gentile businessmen began to suffer discrimination. This new cooperative movement, signaled by the founding of Zion's Cooperative Mercantile Institution, almost drove the merchants out of Utah Territory.

But in the early years the development of a trading market in Salt Lake City proved mutually advantageous. Whether or not the trading turned out to be even depended on many factors including the travelers' haste to get to the nuggets of California or the pioneers' degree of craving for refined goods and clothing. There were high prices for some goods and animals the travelers needed, but there were also high prices for special articles desired by the Saints. The written records left by Gentile visitors and Mormon Saints reveal the kind of treatment the travelers received from their Rocky Mountain hosts.

chapter five

SAINTS OR SINNERS?

SOME adventurers thought Salt Lake prices for goods were exorbitant. There was grumbling about the monopoly exercised by the Saints and comments were made that Utah residents were "alive to any means of acquiring wealth,"[1] or they were "eager for a trade provided they can get the best of the bargain."[2] A few felt the Mormons were "very severe with the emigrants who are unlucky enough to have to apply to them for supplies."[3] A. J. McCall commented that they seemed "disposed to make all they can out of us."[4]

There were occasional cases of cupidity or reluctance on the part of a few Mormon traders to declare all the facts. Madison Moorman recorded how his company was sold defective canteens by a swindling Mormon tinner and then had to hire someone else to re-solder the containers.[5] As for sinning by omitting to tell all, the classic story was Priddy Meeks' tale about a horse trade he made. Meeks had joined the Mormon church in 1840 in Illinois where he practiced doctoring as "an anti-poison [medicine] man." After crossing the plains to Utah in 1847, he settled in Salt Lake City until 1851. Then he moved to Parowan, Utah, where his spouse of twenty-five years insisted he take another wife. In his confession of the trade of a less than superior horse to an eager traveler, he recorded in his journal:

> I had an indian pony mare with a colt, she was in splendid order but the laziest animal I ever owned. I rode her two or three times but I could not get her out of a walk. I tried her with a switch and club and spured her until the blood ran down her sides but all to no purpose. I tied up the colt and took her to the emigrants. The colt being absent made her act like a smart animal. They liked her looks well because she would hold her head high and show full of life. What is your price says the man? I said I have no price but that I wanted clothing for my family which was five in number.

I believe his heart was softened for he handed out goods, some ready made, and some not, until we all had two suits each from top to toe, both shoes and stockings and everything that was needed. He said how much more? I said, hand out and I will tell you when to stop. He handed out factory and calico until I was almost ashamed even my conscience reminded me of stopping. I said, "here is a great coat and a high pair of boots for winter," and he handed them out without a word. I had them priced as well as I could after he left. We thought that they amounted to about $80.00 or $100.00.[6]

Some of the Saints even forgot their obligation to pay to their church the required ten percent tithing from favorable transactions they concluded with California-bound wayfarers. Goudy Hogan was circumspect in this regard and turned in to his bishop a shotgun for which he had traded with an emigrant, although he kept the "riffle" that was a part of the deal.[7] But Benjamin Johnson had a real struggle with his soul as a result of some nice bargains in cows he had gotten from passing travelers. His church contribution was called for. But he was now getting along so nicely he felt "too poor and Stingy to pay my tithing." Every time he visited his corral he reminded himself that he should deliver an especially promising animal to his bishop but he failed to do so. One morning the cow died suddenly just outside the corral so Johnson, angry with himself, at once took an ox to pay his tithing. "I knew it was of the Lord to give me a lesson I needed . . . an experience for others to shun."[8]

Most travelers commented on the reasonable prices offered by the Salt Lake pioneers for goods or draft animals, and expressions abound that attest to the kindness and hospitality offered to eastern visitors. "The Mormons were very good to us," wrote Jacob Storey.[9] H. S. Brown commented, "I was never treated better than by those people."[10] Jane Richards, whose husband had been sent from home to serve three years as a church missionary leaving her to make her own living, began braiding straw hats and charged only a dollar apiece. Her customers were surprised because the hats were so inexpensive. "In all our dealings with emigrants," she said, "we took no advantage of them."[11]

Captain Stansbury, after a year in Salt Lake City, judiciously evaluated Mormon dealings with the emigrants. His favorable account must be tempered by the fact that as a government official he was treated with special consideration and the utmost respect. He thought the Mormon people were ever fair and upright with the passing emigrants, did not take unfair advantage of them and sold whatever supplies they could spare at moderate prices. In his official report he wrote that he did not know of a single instance of fraud or extortion practiced on an emigrant and that any such charges "arose either from interested misrepresentation or erroneous information." The few travelers arrested for breaking municipal laws he thought deserved the treatment they received. He felt that the community of the Saints was, in every respect, quiet, orderly, and industrious.[12]

When historian Dale Morgan published eight "Letters by Forty-Niners," he noted that seven writers were favorable in their accounts while only one was antagonistic.[13] Unfavorable comments, when they were made, were usually directed against church leaders, especially Brigham Young, and not the Mormon people. Langworthy, for example, recorded an account of a sermon by Young forbidding emigrants from taking any wheat from the valley with the threat that if they tried to do so they would be pursued and returned and "made to smart for it. . . ."[14] On the other hand, Young told a group of assembled emigrants that if they caught one of his followers stealing their property, "shoot him dead on the spot, and all this people will say, Amen."[15] At another time he warned his members that if they were discovered speculating to the disadvantage of their brethren and did not repent they would go to hell "and that a low one. . . ."[16] Lorenzo Brown reported that Young's condemnation of Mormons who tried to speculate off the emigrants by exchanging fat oxen for poor ones was also strong.[17] Perhaps a *Deseret News* report on July 6, 1850, of a sermon by Brigham Young best represented his insistence on fair dealings with visitors:

> There are hundreds of emigrants now coming here, destitute: I say to you, Latter-day Saints, let no man go hungry from your doors; divide with them, and trust in God for more; . . . I say treat every man kindly, and especially if there is any prospect of helping them on their journey. Emigrants, don't let your spirits be worn down; and shame be to the door where a man has to go hungry away.

More serious charges were directed against the Mormons of the Great Basin. These stemmed from rumors about conflicts between Mormons and non-Mormons in the Mississippi Valley. As early as

1846, emigrants were choosing to travel the route south of the Platte River to avoid so-called warlike Mormons who were allegedly planning to murder travelers and seize their property.[18] In 1847, wild tales also circulated that the Mormon pioneers intended to ally themselves with three Indian tribes and kill and loot along the trail. A *New York Tribune* correspondent in October of 1849 thought that "if these people were such thieves and robbers as their enemies represented them in the States, I must think they have greatly reformed in point of industry since coming to the mountains."[19] Emigrant Sheldon Young also found the Saints to be industrious and hard working, despite the alarming rumors and "scare-crow stories" he had heard about them.[20] H. B. Taylor, a disgruntled Latter-day Saint, was excommunicated for spreading falsehoods that Apostle Ezra Taft Benson and other leaders intended to "kill strangers & take their cattle and other property and many other such things."[21]

Much of the anti-Mormon feeling came from opposition to the theology and practices of the new religion, and at least some of the emigrants were forthright enough to say so. One traveler had thought, before reaching Utah, that the Mormons had been an abused people. He discovered that "the earth does not produce so degraded, so damnable a community of people" because of their disregard of morality in practicing polygamy.[22] This charge seemed to lie behind the dislike of many of the emigrants, one of whom, W. S. McBride, finally dismissed all Mormons as like the "canting Round Heads of Cromwells' time."[23]

A persistent rumor frightened many argonauts. Mormon agents were supposedly at work among the Indians turning them against all Gentile companies, who often faced prairie grass fires set by marauding bands.[24] Twenty-five members of the Delaware Mining Company wrote the *Deseret News* on June 25, 1849, that although they had been warned by a French-Canadian at Fort Laramie that the Saints were inciting Indians against emigrants, the report proved to be quite false and the tribes were entirely friendly. Charles Ferguson's group received assurances from Mormon leaders that the Paiutes along the trail to Los Angeles were peaceable because their noble chief and the entire tribe had been baptized into the church of the Latter-day Saints and had thus "secured through tickets and a front seat in the happy hunting grounds of the hereafter. . . ."[25] Accusations of Mormon complicity in arousing Indians against Gentile settlers and travelers continued for thirty years but these charges were evidently groundless during the gold rush.

The most common complaint by emigrants was that the Mormon people were "seceders and vain-glorious pretenders"[26]who used their persecutions in the Midwest as an excuse to "bid open defience to the United States, her government and her people."[27] This supposed abuse of Uncle Sam and the denial of the authority of the American government led some travelers to claim that the Mormon leaders intended to bring all nations under their control.[28] Many of the adventurers from Illinois and Missouri, either through fear or prejudice, detoured around Salt Lake City by way of Fort Hall. Travelers from other sections of the nation, intrigued by a visit to the home of the strange Mormons, deliberately chose a route through Salt Lake.[29] These fearless adventurers reported being well treated[30] but did find the Latter-day Saints rather sore towards the United States[31] for not protecting them at Nauvoo. They also discovered that the fears of the people from Missouri and Illinois were not unfounded because if they had been recognized "they would surely have been tried and executed."[32] At least Jerome Howard thought so, while Thomas Evershed considered that perhaps as far as the Missouri and Illinois troubles were concerned, the Mormons were as much sinned against as sinning.[33]

Visitors to Salt Lake City found the Saints quite amiable unless reminded of their persecution which immediately aroused their ire. "They are all, large & small, male & female, unanimous in their hatred to an Illinoisan & Missourian,"[34] "for whom they indulge the most bitter hatreds, and cultivate a spirit of revenge; invoking curses upon them even to the fourth generation."[35] Lieutenant Gunnison pointed out that perhaps individual Saints made excessive threats against their former persecutors, but their leaders were more restrained and wiser, at least publicly.[36]

There were many instances of reciprocity between the Mormons and their visitors.[37] Dr. Thomas Flint had traded some provisions to a group of needy Saints on the Overland Trail. When he arrived in Salt Lake City his act of kindness had not been forgotten and he was well treated by his newfound friends.[38] Another emigrant, George Blodgett, received assistance from four Mormons who volunteered to travel two hundred miles back along the trail to help him recover four mules and seven horses stolen from him. After an adventurous and successful retrieval of the purloined animals, one of the Mormons recorded, "He bade us farewell, said we had treated him as a gentleman."[39] And William Lorton became such a friend of the family with whom he boarded that when he left his host gave him "a blessing & wished that plenty of gold might be my portion. . . ."[40] Indeed, a number of former "mobocrats" who dared to venture into Salt Lake City received the same hospitality other gold diggers did, according to Mormon Eli Kelsey.[41]

Of all the help offered by valley residents to needy travelers, none was more appreciated than the care given to those stricken with "mountain fever" or the more dreaded scourge, cholera. In 1849 there were almost 2,000 deaths along the stretch of road between Independence and Fort Laramie (a mortality rate approaching six percent); in 1850 2,500 died. Many pioneers turned back to the Missouri River.[42] B. F. Dowell reported the return of a disillusioned gold-rusher who "had seen the elephant, and eaten its ears."[43] Ill travelers who had passed the halfway point on the journey hoped to avoid "the sight of grave diggers" along every mile of the trail and to get nursing care from a Christian family of Mormons in Salt Lake.[44] Some companies or ill argonauts who had determined to take Sublette's Cutoff changed course and headed for the haven of the Mormon city.[45]

There they found a healthy community. Many residents had been comparatively free from illness on their journeys to Utah. Travelers testified that while cholera struck along the south side of the Platte River, the Mormon Trail on the north side remained relatively free from the disease.[46] As for life on the shores of Great Salt Lake, Brigham Young reported in late 1849 that "the health of the Saints in the Valley is good, and it is so seldom that anyone dies we scarce recollect when such an event last occured." A year later Young announced there had been a few deaths, "mostly of emigrants."[47] John Pulsipher explained that good health was the result of the spartan diet forced on the Saints. In later years when food became abundant, Utahns supposedly began to succumb to illnesses because they ate too much of a variety of foods "which clogs the stomach & brings on disease."[48]

Seriously ill overlanders seeking help at Salt Lake were fortunate if they found a home with a wife or mother skilled, from practical experience, in nursing an invalid back to good health. The doctors along the trail and the valley were best avoided by the knowledgeable travelers. A young man wrote his father, "If a fellow gets sick, he might as well blow his brains out at once,"[49] and the Latter-day Saints preferred calling on their elders to pray for them. The favorite dosages of calomel, laudanum, camphor, and brandy prescribed by frontier physicians[50] and withholding cool drinking water in cases of fever did not lend itself to speedy recoveries.[51] Priddy Meeks became so successful at "doctoring" that he took up the practice of Thompsonian medicine (curing with herbs) and applied his skills on trusting emigrants who sought him out. From their tents pitched along City Creek "in a row like so many geese," they came to him for a cure from mountain fever. He had them "jump all over in the City Creek and crawl back into their tent and cover up warm...." The treatment seemed to work. Although he could have cheated and defrauded these strangers in the fees he collected, he wrote that he did not do so and "kept a clear conscience." He received their expressions of gratitude when they left.

Gentile and Mormon journals agree that sick and helpless travelers were taken in and treated with the utmost kindness and sent on their way "rejoicing" to California[52] "where they might dig gold to their Hearts Content."[53] Most were grateful, especially when "perfectly helpless and incapable of being taken any further," as was a member of Beeson Townsend's party.[54] Companies were usually solicitous in making arrangements for the care of an ill comrade but Brigham Young was forced to comment in late 1850, "Several have arrived in our city, who had been left, by their companions to die by the way side...."[55] One of the fortunate was young John Hudson. "Gentleman" Hudson almost died before reaching Salt Lake where "to my surprise and gratitude, I met a pious, kind, and intelligent artist, and a countryman also, who took me, emaciated, sick, and dirty, to his humble home...." After his health was restored he remained in the valley during the winter. Eventually he joined the Mormon church and lived in Utah until his death in December 1850.[56]

Sick travelers who did not recover were buried at the hands of the church with the various Mormon families involved preparing shrouds and coffins.[57] Philip Schuyler, for example, died in Salt Lake City on July 26, 1850, and was interred "in the Mormon grave yarde in a parte for the emagrants" where twenty-five other travelers had already been buried.[58] After two years of caring for ill and deceased adventurers, the first presidency of the church offered a mild complaint in the *Deseret News* of March 22, 1851: "Hitherto, California emigrants have been accustomed to leave their sick on our hands, at a heavy expense, and depart without notice. . . ." They suggested that the California and Oregon emigrants of 1851 consider another route to the Pacific Coast.

Trading disagreements, allegations about disloyalty to the government, or disputes about the care of needy travelers did not inspire the disgruntlement emigrants and settlers both felt when the law intervened. Church administration of justice was apparently sufficient until December 26, 1848, when the church High Council adopted a series of five local ordinances: (1) vagabonds were to be put to work cultivating the soil; (2) disorderly persons could be punished with thirty-nine lashes or fines at the discretion of the judges; (3) those guilty of adultery or fornication were to receive thirty-nine lashes or fines up to $1,000; (4) thieves and housebreakers were to receive thirty-nine lashes and be expected to restore any property taken fourfold; and (5) persons convicted of drunkenness, swearing, cursing, etc., could be fined up to $25.[59] The whippings were to be administered in public at a post on which a bell had been hung, but they were never well received by either the culprit or onlookers and apparently only a few were conducted. The High Council continued to pass ordinances until December 29, 1849, and exercised considerable authority. But during the years of the gold rush, the recognized legal authority came to be the new State of Deseret, which the Mormon leaders expected would be accepted by the Congress of the United States.[60]

This new state came into being as the result of a convention held on March 5, 1849, followed by an election accepting the new state constitution and selecting a slate of officers headed by Brigham Young as governor. The fifteen senators and thirty representatives organized their respective houses in July, and the First Legislative Session began December 3, 1849, and ended March 2, 1850. A memorial was addressed to Congress asking admission as a state. It was not until January 1850 that the Legislature established a judiciary for the new State of Deseret, organized the area into six counties, and passed other laws and regulations. Thus, throughout the second year of the gold rush, Salt Lake Valley was under a government not recognized by the United States Congress. Finally, under the Compromise of 1850, Congress established the Territory of Utah on September 9, 1850, although Brigham Young did not take the oath of office as governor until February 3, 1851. It was perhaps understandable that emigrants criticized Utah's government, which was in a state of flux and under direct Mormon control throughout the two-year period when gold diggers were passing through Salt Lake City.[61]

The union of church and state in the Great Basin led to affairs going "strictly hand-in-hand," and to an execution of "justice without authority."[62] This judicial system was deplored by some travelers but accepted with equanimity by most residents. The Saints saw nothing wrong with having the laws promulgated from the pulpit each Sabbath,[63] and rested in the security of a patriarchal and theocratic society which permitted them to sleep at night "with no protection from midnight molestation other than a wagon-cover of linen and the aegis of the law."[64] To many it seemed that the new emigration threatened such protection. When the *Deseret News* began to note robberies of the McVicar & Barlow Watch Shop, of a break-in of William's and Blair's store, and of a theft from the McKean & Barlow establishment,[65] it seemed quite plausible for one Mormon diarist to add, "Two California Emigrants have been arrested & brought to trial. One was liberated & the other fined $200."[66] By June 1850, an incipient crime wave led Brigham Young to organize a police force of forty officers who accepted their twenty-five-cents-an-hour positions as a mission to keep the peace and "put down iniquity when ever we find it...." After blessing them in the name of the Lord Jesus Christ, the Mormon leader gave his final instruction: "If any man askes for your authority knock him down with your cane. Serve my Boys the same way—..."[67]

One of the most common infractions of city law was the trespass of stock in grain fields and home gardens. As early as May 12, 1849, the High Council assessed a fine of a dollar a head for cattle or horses running at large in the valley.[68] The inadequately fenced fields and gardens only added to the problem,[69] which worsened with the arrival of thousands of emigrants. One party had to pay $74 to the local court when their cattle destroyed two gardens.[70] Shortly after this incident, a city ordinance with eleven sections was enacted to control branding and estrays and to assess damages caused by loose stock.[71] McDiarmid, who was fined five dollars for damages caused by his horses, complained that it was the practice of some Mormon "swindlers" to drive traveler's stock off at night to the estray pen and pocket one fourth of the fines collected.[72] And Thomas Flint, forced to pay a fine of $20 for damages inflicted on a stack of wheat by his horses, recorded for posterity that the local justice of the peace threatened to double the amount *"if he found fault or swore."*[73]

Stansbury was convinced that those who stole or trespassed on the rights of the community deserved the fines and punishments meted out to them as would have happened in any civilized area of the nation.[74] Cynical Jerome Howard thought that in their conception of property rights the Saints differed very little from other places where each one "gets what he can and keeps what he gets." Offenders against property received harsh sentences in the new Zion.[75] Vincent Hoover and John Hudson were certain that a thief was either shot or forfeited his head.[76] Actual sentences for theft were more in line with the one given a man convicted of stealing a pair of boots. He was forced to pay the owner four times the worth of the boots plus a fifty-dollar fine and all court costs.[77] If a convicted person could not pay the fine, he was sentenced to work on the road and was encumbered by a ball and chain.[78]

A common practice was to sentence serious offenders to up to two years of servitude by auctioning them off to the highest bidder— a novel means of disposing of offenders since there was no prison.[79] William Lorton described in detail an auction he observed where three boys were sold for having picked thirty dollars from the pocket of a dusty adventurer while he was bathing in the Jordan River:

> the first was a small boy, . . . he had a very rogish countenance for a youth & kept grining while the marshal cryed out going, going. . . . at first there was no bidding, but finally it rose to 1 doll & then to 2 he was then struck off to the bidder. . . . he had served 1 year before on a similar offense, his benefactors or guardians could not make a mormon of him or make him come to prayers, till one night his pious preceptor endeavored by the rod to make him come to his prayers, & got him down on his knees, but would not pray for he said he couldnt, say anything said his master accompanying his command with a blow. "Amen" cryed the boy & up he jumped.[80]

In the same proceeding a fourth boy was sold for six dollars for passing a counterfeit five-dollar bill.

Usually purchasers of these wayward individuals had to post bond for their good behavior.[81] Overlander W. B. Taylor recorded the auction of a boy whose only crime was being an orphan. The purchaser had to give bond stating he would give his new possession proper care and treatment and three months schooling each year. At first Taylor was upset by the affair's similarity to southern auction blocks for slaves, but he finally rationalized that the Mormons were correct in ensuring that unattended boys did not turn into hoodlums or street Arabs.[82] Salt Lake laws and punishments were primitive but not far removed from similar practices found in other frontier areas at the time.

The union of church and state gave considerable authority to the church's bishop's courts to decide temporal as well as spiritual matters, and the arrival of many quarreling gold diggers in the valley tended to strengthen the determination of the Mormon leaders to avoid litigation among their followers. On June 2, 1850, the elders of one congregation settled the matter of the ownership of a horse by discussing the case during Sabbath meeting "to save the time, expense & hard feelings of a long and tedious lawsuit. . . ." Brigham Young commended the action and advised the members to follow this course until an individual refused to accept a church verdict and insisted on taking his case to a civil court.[83] Willard Snow emphasized his President's counsel by defining, in the *Deseret News* of August 10, 1850, the different responsibilities of the bishops' courts and the common courts. If any Saint transgressed the laws of his church, he was to be disfellowshiped and be "delivered over as a citizen unto the laws of the land." No citizen of the state was answerable to church law, but church members were "amenable to both church and state for the rectitude of their conduct."

A few months later, on February 22, 1851, the editor of the newspaper recounted the case of a Mormon who initiated a suit against a fellow church member through a civil magistrate. When the judge learned that the would-be litigant had not taken the "gospel steps" of trying to settle the matter before a church council, he refused to allow the civil action until this first procedure had been exhausted. Not until the accused brother had been disfellowshiped or excommunicated would the judge "let loose the law upon him." Only the lawless and disobedient were to be haled before a court. But at times Patriarch Young was less than satisfied with the judicial acumen and performance of his bishops. One was relieved of his duties "because the Dimes had began to blind his eyes." Brigham Young threatened at one time to send one bishop on a foreign mission "in order to save him,"[84] and remarked on another occasion that the bishops "are not fit to decide a case between two old women, let alone two men."[85]

With the organization of the State of Deseret, judicial practice became more formal. Twenty justices of the peace were chosen to decide civil and minor criminal cases. The jurisdiction of each precinct coincided with the nineteen ecclesiastical ward boundaries, and a twentieth jurisdiction was set up for the North Cottonwood district.[86] Other justices were apparently added to the original list because Hosea Stout, who is one of the best sources, also described litigating cases under Aaron F. Farr, Willard Snow, and Zerubbabel Snow. In addition to Stout, Henry G. Sherwood and William Wines Phelps were prominent attorneys involved in cases concerned with emigrant troubles.[87] Governor Young, in his annual message of December 2, 1850, noted that not a single case had been reported for adjudication before either the county or supreme court. He thought this favorable result had been achieved because the justices of the peace had been instructed to compromise differences instead of trying to promote litigation.[88]

Despite this rose-colored review by the governor, the justices and lawyers involved in the emigrant court fights during the gold rush years came to be heartily tired of cases that could drag on until midnight or 1:00 A.M. Once a case lasted until 8:00 A.M. the next morning.[89] Forty-niner John Hudson, who worked as clerk to one of the prominent justices during the summer of 1850, recalled that the emigrants were "contentious to a shocking extent" and were so litigious that they pursued their disputes "to extremities." According to him, the court forced the antagonists to pay "pretty heavily for costs" to ensure proper remuneration for the cases.[90] Hosea Stout was kept so busy that by the last of July he was ill and "worn out with Lawing. . . ."[91] At first the court actions were quite a novelty to the peace-minded Saints, but soon their leaders were advising "cease contention, and starve the judges and lawyers."[92] The church called upon the disputatious adventurers to settle their own difficulties or even better, to have no difficulties at all.

John Hudson's recently-discovered "Letters" give this young Englishman's impressions of the courthouse and the procedures followed by the court:

> This is called the Bowery and is used for all publick meetings. The scenes that transpire are very characteristic of Americanism and would make you accustomed to the form of an English Court of Justice smile at its oddity. We gather round a deal table, the Magistrate, for the weather is hot, with his coat off, sits amongst Constables, Attorneys and prisoners and, for further convenience rests his legs by sticking them on the table, kindly affording the throng of lookers on an opportunity of ascertaining the health of his soles. During the progress of the case, pretty much all are industriously engaged in whittling, grievously to the detriment of table and benches which they slice without the least compunction. The dresses of the newly arived emigrants are often picturesque while the easy colloquial manner in which business is transacted makes a novel scene but all this does not interfere with the administration of justice in righteousness and in maj[ority] is honest clear headed and impartial.[93]

The most common suit at law concerned the division of property. Companies completing a "quarreling journey" from the Missouri proceeded to abandon well-intentioned constitutions and by-laws, and individual members sought the means to continue on to California in their own ways or with another group.[94] Occasionally cases were settled out of court, but many bickered right down to the last piece of hardtack and pint of beans. Hosea Stout was involved in many cases. He disgustedly recorded one day, "Disputes are arising among the emergrants . . . while they appeal to the law for a redress of grievances & division of property which is not very interisting to relate."[95]

Some trains of emigrants broke up before the travelers reached Salt Lake and anger mounted as lawyers and judges tried to defuse explosive situations. Glenn & Co.'s large train distintegrated at Independence Rock with some of the passengers threatening to shoot one of the leaders while twenty-five others bought oxen from a nearby government freight outfit and left on their own. Later four of the Glenn party who refused to surrender property under court attachment at Salt Lake City were fined from fifty to one hundred dollars each for abusing officers and resisting arrest. Hosea Stout, as one of the attorneys involved, wrote of the four defendants, "They manifested a hostile spirit in the main and H. [Holloway] even laughed [at] the court in contempt at first, but they all appeared very pious after the decision of the Court."[96]

After suits concerning the division of property, the greatest number of difficulties among the gold-rushers centered around breaches of contract. A few were settled out of court, but most had to be adjudicated by a justice of the peace with amounts ranging from $50 to $163.75 being awarded the injured parties.[97] Vincent Hoover's company paid off a driver who sued for his wages by giving the man a fifteen-dollar "wach."[98] Another was convicted of deserting a customer at Pacific Springs. Being fresh out of funds, he was obliged to work out his fine of $145 and costs under the supervision of Sister Charles C. Rich.[99] A man named Martin was instructed by the court to take his client on to California. Instead, Martin left in the night. The local sheriff traveled thirty miles beyond Brownsville to apprehend him but returned empty-handed when the Strother train of sixty people, which Martin had joined, refused to allow him to be taken into custody.[100] In another typical case, a lawsuit was instituted against two men for failing to take a third to the gold fields. The defendant claimed he had already brought them to California because Utah was part of California. The judge ruled that the wily guide would have to refund half the passage money. Emigrant John Wood, who observed the proceedings, ridiculed the "gass-eloquence and technical ingenuity" of the attorneys involved.[101]

There were, of course, cases of theft. One required the sheriff to lead a posse two hundred miles into the western desert to capture some robbers who had made off with an entire outfit belonging to an overland party.[102] Suits concerning horse stealing appeared prominently on the court dockets. John Y. Green refused to deliver a horse to its rightful owner when instructed by the court and became so abusive he was fined an additional $50 for contempt.[103] In an especially "very excited & turbulent" case, Hosea Stout represented an emigrant named Kenicoot whose wagon and outfit were lost in a crossing on Weber River by Francis Drake and some other travelers who had set themselves up as ferry operators. They had insured safe passage of the wagon but now refused to compensate the owner for his loss of $75. When the ferrymen learned that other customers were about to sue, they "concluded to pay up and be off."[104]

Sadder cases concerning the sick and deceased occurred. E. C. Dougherty was finally acquitted of the charge of leaving a passenger "sick, to perish on the road." The local justices were sometimes forced to become involved in supervising the disposition of the last effects of those who had died on the trail or at Salt Lake City, although usually an emigrant party was considerate enough not to quarrel over the possessions of departed friends.[105]

Assault and battery cases and violations of local ordinances were handled with dispatch. Matthias Weaver sued Joseph Phillipson for a beating he had suffered at Green River Ferry but was surprised when, after an investigation, the justice fined him $5 and his assailant $10.[106] Litigants involved in breaches of the peace usually received modest fines of from $3 to $5; however, the Reverend Alvin Musset of Missouri was assessed a $10 fine and $15 in damages plus costs for forcibly taking his cattle from the stray pen where they had been legally impounded while "repeatedly placing his hand on his pistol." Attorney Stout thought he was a "perfect specimen of the Missouri ministry."[107]

Gold-rushers traveling by way of Salt Lake were more successful in replenishing their larders during 1849 when there was a bounteous harvest. A greater number of settlers and emigrants in 1850 were forced to divide a smaller yield of food stocks. Nevertheless, in both years, as fair-minded visitors like Stansbury and Gunnison attested, the Mormon pioneers were generous and just in their treatment of the exhausted wayfarers. Prices for supplies and services were reasonable, hospitality flourished in Mormon homes, and those pilgrims who were ill were taken in and cared for. Salt Lake City offered the only court system between the Missouri River and California to adjudicate the legal problems encountered during the journey. Travelers received impartial justice at the hands of Mormon judges and lawyers. Despite a few dissatisfied patrons whose anti-Mormon sentiments or adverse sentences and fines led to later published recriminations, most emigrant journals record an acceptance of Mormon justice.

The emigrant litigation reached new heights between June and August of 1850 when attorneys like Hosea Stout were kept busy from seven in the morning until midnight representing their contentious clients. Most cases dealt with the distribution of property as the various companies broke up; the next most numerous lawsuits were concerned with breach of contract. There were assault and battery cases, although emigrant accounts are remarkably free of incidents involving serious violence. Probably the most irritating suits, to the travelers, were brought by the local Mormon officials for trespass on local grain fields or gardens. The Mormon leaders finally tired of the litigious strife introduced into their peaceful society and began to announce that they hoped the hungry gold seekers would travel the Fort Hall route. But during the two main gold rush years of 1849 and 1850 their courts provided a real service. In between the bartering sessions and interminable court cases there were periods when travelers could observe the strange and exotic customs and sights of Mormondom, and most emigrants took full advantage of this once-in-a-lifetime opportunity.

FIG. 1. Fort Bridger on Black's Fork of the Green River in 1849–50. For the few forty-niners who chose the trail via Fort Bridger, there was an easy eighty-five-mile stretch on to Fort Hall with good grass forage along the way. *Courtesy of the Utah State Historical Society.*

FIG. 2. Bridger's Ferry was one of many river crossings along the Overland Trail. In the spring, Brigham Young sent out church members to establish and operate ferries, and many gold seekers encountered their first Mormons at these river crossings. *Courtesy of the Utah State Historical Society.*

FIG. 3. Fort Hall in 1849. With the pioneering of Hudspeth's Cutoff, wagon traffic by-passed Fort Hall reducing travel time for argonauts anxious to get to the goldfields. *Courtesy of the Utah State Historical Society.*

FIG. 4. Lithograph of the first view of the Salt Lake Valley. The journey down Big Mountain could only be accomplished by taking off all the oxen but the wheelers, which were yoked to the wagon tongue, and locking all the wheels. *Courtesy of the Utah State Historical Society.*

FIG. 5. Engraving of Great Salt Lake City in 1853. In 1849 gold-rushers found 6,000 to 7,000 people living in the wilderness city. *Courtesy of the Historical Department, Church of Jesus Christ of Latter-day Saints.*

Fig. 6. An early view of Main Street, Salt Lake City. Forty-niners found habitations primitive—log cabins, wagon boxes, "or just a few pieces of lumber set end-ways . . . with a sheet across each end . . . for a door." *Courtesy of the Utah State Historical Society.*

FIG. 7. The Old Salt Lake Tabernacle about 1855. *Courtesy of the Utah State Historical Society.*

FIGS. 8 AND 9. An original pencil sketch and finished lithograph of early Salt Lake done by John Hudson. The lithograph appeared in Stansbury's *Exploration and Survey of the Great Salt Lake Valley of Utah. Courtesy of Marriott Library, University of Utah.*

FIG. 10. Church president and Governor Brigham Young was a very gregarious person who visited the emigrant camps and kept an open door at his home. Howard Stansbury may have been the first to compare Young to the prophet Moses after he had led the pioneers "through the wilderness to a remote and unknown land." The Mormons gave Brigham Young their wholehearted loyalty and trust. *Courtesy of the Utah State Historical Society.*

FIG. 11. Some pilgrims took the opportunity to visit the Great Salt Lake, but most travelers missed the beaches on the south shore and passed only marshes and mudflats when they took the Salt Lake Road that ran east of the lake. *Courtesy of the Utah State Historical Society.*

FIG. 12. A rare early photograph of the Bear River Bridge near Colliston, Utah, that replaced the ferry. Nelson Slater accused the Mormon leaders of encouraging travel on the Salt Lake Road to make a profit off ferriage, which he claimed was as high as $8 for a wagon and team. *Gift of Jack Scott Chivers, Helena, Mont., to Mr. and Mrs. Brigham D. Madsen.*

FIG. 13. Fort Utah on the Provo River in 1850. Fort Utah was forty miles south of Salt Lake and was the last civilized outpost on the southern route to Los Angeles. *Courtesy of the Historical Department, Church of Jesus Christ of Latter-day Saints.*

chapter six

TAKING IN THE SIGHTS

AFTER taking care of certain matters like gorging on fresh vegetables, buying and trading for animals and equipment, and dividing up company property, the tired and dusty pilgrims wanted to clean up before taking in the sights, so they headed for the warm springs about a mile north of Salt Lake City. The springs filled a pool twenty feet square and fifteen inches deep with crystal-clear water, and green, black, and yellow pebbles covered the bottom. Water temperature was 105 degrees and a perpetual cloud of vapor hung over the pool. After the initial shock, travelers found the water comfortable for bathing. As many as twenty people could bathe at one time, and diary entries attest to how fascinating these warm springs were for Saint and Gentile alike.[1]

Two days after the arrival of the original Mormon pioneers, Brigham Young and a party bathed in the pool and found its waters "very pleasant and refreshing."[2] The gold-rushers described their baths in superlatives: "perfectly delicious," indescribable luxury," "glorious," until a more prosaic Saint laconically noted a "good wash."[3] Neighboring Mormons called it the "pool of Siloam" after the Biblical spring outside of Jerusalem.[4] The waters were impregnated with sulfur, and William Johnston, after about fifteen minutes in the water, "felt a sickening sensation." He was told this feeling could be avoided by bathing before sunrise or after sunset.[5] The sulfur content precluded the use of soap, but Charles Gray found this no impediment to getting clean: "We were all in the dustiest state imaginable & 15 minutes brought us out all white again."[6]

To many the warm springs were more important for their healing properties. The emigrants noted that the Mormons attributed their good health in part to the waters, which were looked upon as "a panacea for diseases in general"[7] and as a cure for "the most inveterate case of rheumatism."[8] Some Saints declared that they came to the valley perfect cripples but had regained their health and agility by immersing themselves.[9] The editor of the *Frontier Guardian* in Kanesville, Iowa, beseeched financial help on March 20, 1850, for a Brother Stoddard so that he could make the journey to Salt Lake Valley and "wash in that warm pool . . . where the first that step in are healed of whatsoever disease they have." Emigrants were also interested in the curative properties of the springs. In a typical incident the company of John Benson placed two sick members in the pool, rubbed them down well, and left them to soak. The invalids declared themselves much better, although Benson suspected the two mostly wanted to make their nurses feel good.[10]

Many of the eastern wayfarers realized the springs were a valuable possession. Charles Gray was certain "the owner or lessee would realize a fortune from it, half a million wouldn't purchase it in Europe I am confident."[11] Brigham Young might have been a rustic in the view of some travelers, but he was a cagey rustic. He was instrumental in having the legislature of the State of Deseret appropriate $6,000 to construct a public bathhouse.[12] Drusilla Hendricks' family was given the responsibility of erecting the building, which had twelve rooms in the front. The warm water was carried a third of a mile from the spring through pump logs laboriously bored through the center.[13] The building, which was "one of the greatest luxuries known in any country,"[14] was formally dedicated by Prophet and Governor Young on November 27, 1850. Elder and Lieutenant Governor Heber C. Kimball offered the dedicatory prayer that "the water might be filled with life and health, . . . and that no foul spirit might ever pass the threshold. . . ."[15] Advertised rates were $1.00 for families of from two to four persons up to $3.50 for families of from sixteen to twenty-four persons.[16] By decree, Tuesdays and Fridays were reserved as women's days with the other days for men, "and no peeping Toms allowed."[17] While Dow Stephens and his fellow emigrants were enjoying the luxurious waters one day, a man drove up in a wagon and informed them that this was ladies bath day whereupon the gold seekers, declaring they were "entirely ignorant of the rules," donned their clothes and left.[18]

Almost three miles north of the warm springs was a hot spring that could cook meat placed in it.[19] Scientifically-oriented James Hutchings used a thermometer and determined the temperature was 122 degrees.[20] More than one curious visitor who tested the water with his hand would have agreed with John Lewis—"Without being told I jurked it back."[21]

Bathing in Great Salt Lake did not receive much notice because only a few parties chose to travel to California by way of Hastings Cutoff south of the lake where there were the best beaches. The road along the east shore passed marshy and muddy areas unsuitable for swimming. The Hastings travelers usually noted the Mormon entrepreneur who had established a saltery on the south shore where he was converting three or four gallons of water into one of salt, or three of brine into two of salt, depending on which journal one reads.[22] Most citizens usually got their year's supply by shoveling it up off the beach as one would shovel sand.[23] Adventurers took dips in the lake, whose water was clear as crystal, and marveled, as do today's visitors, that it was "strong enough to bear one up without the least effort being made...."[24]

After a bath and shave, the visitors from the east looked forward to attending the Sabbath day services of the Latter-day Saints. Most went out of curiosity, but a few were hungering for a good gospel sermon. The course of events followed in the meetings seemed novel to many. William Johnston described in some detail how the services opened with a brass band playing. Then a hymn was sung by a "choir of both sexes."[25] An opening prayer followed. Then, a member of the church's twelve apostles took care of some secular matters: a list of articles lost and found during the past week was announced; the names of sick people were read; and assignments were made for work on public projects like digging ditches, building fences, and grading streets.[26] People who had demonstrated outstanding progress in their farming ventures were commended. "A black list [followed] enumerating the idle, slothful, and unimproving portion of the community, who were ... threatened ... to be deprived of their lots, and expelled from the community."[27] Next the names of emigrants who had joined the church were read as well as the names of other travelers who were temporarily resting in Salt Lake City. Then came two or three sermons and a concluding prayer after which the brass band entertained the crowd with waltzes and marches. According to Calvin Taylor, "immediately all was excitement, a confused hum of voices ran through the assembly, friends and acquaintances were interchanging salutes, all was hilarity, and an entire absence of that respectful solemnity common to most temples of worship, strongly reminded one of some holiday occasion when people are wont to collect to indulge in a social intercourse and judging from outward appearances, one would suppose the Mormons to be a happy people."[28] Others agreed that from observing the deportment of the congregation it didn't seem "that any very devotional feeling pervaded them. . . ."[29]

The young men who made up the nearly all-male companies of gold diggers were "almost famished for a sight of bonnets and calicoes." Now they found themselves "afloat, as it were, in a very sea of them."[30] Some of the travelers seemed more interested in the lady members of the congregation with their "rich and becoming costume, each with parasols," than in the biblical pronouncements from the pulpit.[31] William Johnston devoted two full pages of his journal to describing one bewitching young lady but lost interest when a man in the audience placed in her lap "a long gowned, bald-pated, snub-nosed, slobber-mouthed, wriggling, crying baby." He then shifted his attention to "another maiden, the owner of the softest blue eyes imaginable!," but after a long and detailed description of her snowy shoulders, golden hair, and rosy cheeks, it occurred to him that someone might deposit a baby on her lap too. So he squared himself around and paid attention to the services.[32]

The Mormon leaders, former missionaries for their church and accustomed to gospel debate with ministers of other denominations, often invited preachers from among the emigrants to share the pulpit. The Reverend Henry Kroh on one Sunday preached on the text, "Sanctify them through thy truth, thy word is truth," John 17:17.[33] After the Reverend Gresham B. Day spoke to a large congregation, Brigham addressed the crowd, and rather pointedly remembered how Joseph Smith had been ridiculed as a money digger "and now I see hundreds of reverend gentlemen going to dig money."[34] President Young, nevertheless, invited Day to his home where the Baptist minister was "cordially treated."[35]

The Mormon authorities used the summer meetings in the Bowery during 1849 and 1850 to preach the word to visitors and sometimes to good effect. A particularly dynamic testimony might convert members of the audience who would give up their quest for gold and settle in Zion as did Emigrant William Black after being thrilled by a sermon delivered by Apostle John Taylor.[36] Brigham Young led the way but others, like Parley P. Pratt and Lorenzo Snow, were often called upon to preach gospel sermons "intended for use of the Emigrants."[37]

The main theme of the sermons seemed to be anathemas heaped upon the people of Missouri and Illinois for driving the Saints into the mountains of the Great Basin. Said Counselor Heber C. Kimball, "wo unto Missouri, and Illinois" for their murders of little children and the Prophet Joseph Smith.[38] Mormon speakers recalled the "barbarous treatment," and the persecutions and sufferings they had endured.[39] George Jewett reported the meeting he attended: "Several speakers Spoke   they seemed to get very much excited while dwelling upon their wrongs & calling down the vengeance of heaven upon their persecutors   they as a rule declare that if they had a chance they would visit them with the Besom of destruction & destroy them root & branch."[40]

The government was included in the attacks for allowing the persecution. There were many references to the fact that the hunger for California gold would result in the overthrow of the government if its corrupt administrators did not reform.[41] Occasionally a Mormon preacher would get carried away and attack an official like President Zachary Taylor, who did not favor statehood for Deseret, and who should be "in hell begging bread." At this statement "the audience cheered him tremendously."[42] Heber C. Kimball was especially forthright in his denunciations. Once he said that he had been told Congress "was doing nothing but to quarrel & had done nothing for two years but fight & he would to God that they continue to quarrel & kill each other off for two years longer."[43] Of course, not all sermons were attacks on former enemies. Most dealt with religious subjects and with emphasis on the Book of Mormon, which cynic Charles Gray thought "looked as much *like* a Bible as ours, & no doubt will *do these people* about as much good."[44] A. P. Josselyn thought he had heard a good Methodist sermon by a Mormon; Henry Bloom listened to a polemic on the redemption of man which was not of "much account"; John Udell heard some truth and some error; while Robert Bond departed a meeting convinced that the Mormons believed in good works and "were very confident of salvation." Mary Stuart Bailey noted a scolding given by President Young to his followers for teaching that John Wesley and St. Paul had gone "straight to hell when they died." The Prophet advised that if a person did the best he could, the Lord would not send him to serve the Devil.[45]

Perhaps the greatest criticism by easterners of Mormon sermons involved the rough frontier language and plain speech used by some Saints.[46] Langworthy thought that the language would be called profane if heard in the streets.[47] A. J. McCall reported a forceful sermon by Brigham Young concerned with the shortcomings of his people: "for a half hour [Young] delivered a tirade of cant, balderdash and abuse that I would give much if I could report in full." The president "berated soundly the idle drone who chose rather to hang round the street corners and prayer meetings instead of making roads," criticized women for their extravagance and "love of dress and finery," and then "poured out a perfect stream of billingsgate upon the Gentiles, . . . cursed them with bitter curses and called upon God to . . . send them to perdition."[48] It took a strong man to establish the Lord's kingdom in the Utah desert, and the gold-rushers had the privilege of hearing unvarnished facts from the Bowery pupit.

Many travelers discussed the character and personality of the Mormon Prophet. Some saw him only from a distance delivering sermons to large audiences; a few had the opportunity to talk with him in person and fewer still recorded these interviews. To this Moses who had led them "through the wilderness to a remote and unknown land," to give credit to Howard Stansbury who may have been the first to compare Brigham Young to that biblical prophet,[49] the Mormon pioneers gave wholehearted loyalty and trust. For the persecuted Saints, he had been a leader of wisdom and judgment. He had maintained his choice of a home in the Great Basin with unyielding determination despite the starving periods of the first two years of settlement and the golden inducements to lead his people on to California. With the abundant grain harvest of 1849 now cascading from the fields and from the wagon boxes of frantic emigrants, he appeared as a bold prophet whose vision had been firm and true. His followers did not waver in their faith or in his leadership. Saints gave up settled homes in Salt Lake City to accept unquestioningly calls for three or more years of missionary work in the United States and abroad and to establish colonies in the parched desert valleys of Utah and neighboring areas. To the Saints, Brigham Young was the Lion of the Lord; to the California-bound gold diggers he was either a "perfect blackguard" or " a truly good and generous man" depending very much on whether the Gentile visitor saw him only from afar or had the opportunity to feel his drawing power and strength close at hand.[50]

In 1849 Brigham Young was in his forty-eighth year. A New York City newspaper correspondent described him as light complexioned and of ordinary height, but rather corpulent"[51] Dow Stephens years later recalled that in build and in character he was very much like Theodore Roosevelt.[52] As assembled travelers sat in the Bowery and listened to Young's pronouncements, O. J. Hall heard "streams of oaths [which] rolled from his mouth thru discourse."[53] Adam M. Brown thought "his discourses would better grace a butcher's block than a pulpit."[54] Dow Stephens remembered that Young had said "some of you might think I am swearing, but I am not, for when I swear I swear in the name of the Lord, therefore this is not swearing." Stephens added, "Maybe it wasn't swearing, but it sounded much like cursing."[55]

Madison Moorman heard Young speak on the redemption of man in a style he considered affected, weak, unchaste, and pompous. Moorman described the prophet's practical approach to sermonizing by mentioning Young's illustration of the concept of the soul as having the same shape as the body, the latter being only a shell like the peel of an orange, the shell of an egg, or the bark of a tree.[56] On the other hand, William Lorton heard the same kind of pragmatism when the Mormon President advised the emigrants in the audience to fatten their cattle in the valley instead of trading them off at a loss to the Saints and asked "wouldit you bear me out emigrants. the answer was a unanimous yes, a vote of thanks was then given to the Pres. for his disinterested advice. . . ."[57] John Benson reflected that Young "was by all odds the foremost of those who spoke. He is of commanding presence and impressed me as being a strong man."[58]

During the gold rush years, the Mormon kingdom was still small. Brigham Young, as a public figure and a very gregarious person, kept an open door at his home where "a great many comers and goers sit at his table."[59] He also visited the emigrant camps where he "neither interfered with us nor had anything to offer offensive or unpleasant," according to a surprised Charles Ferguson.[60] The Reverend Graham Day thought him "a gentlemen, I think, a Christian. He is very sociable, intelligent, and easy in his bearing."[61] When Missourian Joseph Hamelin visited the Young home, he was told by one of the prophet's wives that the Saints did not trust Missourians. Young later laughed at these fears and assured Hamelin that he would be well treated if he wanted to settle in the valley.[62] A newspaperman from New York found that in private "he is very sociable and talkative, joking and laughing as heartily as anybody."[63] Emigrants often called at the Young residence to say goodbye and thank Young for the good treatment they had received.[64]

His easy sociability did not hide the fact that he was in command of every phase of activity—spiritual and temporal—in Utah. Inveterate anti-Mormon Langworthy was sure that he was virtually a king with the power of life and death over every inhabitant, and that his followers would do anything he proposed because he was worshipped almost as a god.[65] Silas Newcomb expressed to one Saint his surprise at the influence Young exercised over them. The church member replied that " 'should Brigham Young tell him to cut my throat, he should do it' and finished by saying 'that if it was not right, Young would not direct its execution.' "[66] Perhaps the best appraisal of Brigham Young came from Captain Stansbury who had a whole year to form his opinion. Stansbury considered him to be a man of clarity and common sense, aware of the responsibilities of his position, sincere and industrious in his determination to forward the best interests of his people, and utterly courageous in defending them from outside attack. His people gave him their undivided support and confidence and rejoiced when the American President appointed him to be their Territorial Governor. Having shared in their adversities, secure now in the belief that the Mormon settlement was firmly established, and "enthusiastically devoted to the honour and interests of his people, he had won their unlimited confidence, esteem, and veneration, and held an unrivalled place in their hearts." Stansbury felt that despite charges by enemies, Brigham Young's character was above reproach and his integrity unquestioned.[67]

Excursionists arriving in Salt Lake on or near July 24, 1849, were invited to join in the first celebration of the Saints' arrival.[68] Mormons were sensitive to criticism that they were not loyal to their national government, so Brigham Young went to some lengths to explain why his people had not celebrated the Fourth of July. He said that the Declaration of Independence was just as precious to him on the twenty-fourth as it had been twenty days earlier, but that the bread, cucumbers, beets, and other foods would not have been available then for a feast of thanksgiving. Not wishing to celebrate on empty stomachs, he had postponed the holiday until the harvest was ready so they could celebrate both holidays together.[69] There had been no anniversary ceremony the year before because Young and most of the leaders were still in the Iowa settlements and did not arrive back in Salt Lake City until September 20, 1848, where they found a very poor harvest with the people having little to celebrate. The present rich fields of grain in 1849 and the abundance of groceries and manufactured articles brought in by the emigrants now provided the occasion for a pioner day of joy and thankfulness to the Lord.

On the twenty-third, the Saints added an "annex" to the "mud & slates" Bowery.[70] Awnings 100 feet wide were built on each side, and 1,500 lineal feet of tables were constructed of rough boards to hold the bounteous repast. A liberty pole 104 feet high was erected to carry a national flag 65 feet long. A shorter staff was raised to bear the flag that formerly flew from the Nauvoo Temple.[71] A group of California emigrants furnished seventy-five pounds of powder for firing salutes by cannon.[72]

The occasion was so important and symbolic in recognition of the successful establishment of Zion in the mountains that Saints and emigrants by the score recorded the events. An estimated six thousand people thronged to the Bowery along with several hundred emigrants who were invited to join in the celebration.[73] Governor Young was escorted from his residence by a formal military guard and band. Included in the entourage were twelve bishops bearing the banners of their wards; twenty-four young men, each carrying copies of the Declaration of Independence and the Constitution; twenty-four young ladies dressed in white and with wreaths of white roses on their heads, each carrying the Bible and the Book of Mormon; and twenty-four Silver Greys, led by Patriarch Isaac Morley, carrying the American flag. Upon reaching the Bowery the participants in the march paraded around the structure singing hymns while the band played, the cannon and small arms fired, and the assembled multitude shouted "Hosanna to God and the Lamb."[74]

After prayer the program opened with a reading of the Declaration of Independence, with more hymns, and with speeches by six of the leaders. The speakers all referred to the persecutions they had suffered as a people. John Young spoke feelingly of the value of liberty and declared, "Damn the man who shall try to rob us of it."[75] A concomitant theme was that the Saints revered the laws and Constitution of the United States and only denounced the corrupt administrators of the government. The band played some lively airs, hymns were again sung,[76] and then the audience retired to the heavily laden tables where the "whole people then pertook of a rich feast. . . ."[77]

The emigrants did "ample justice to the good dinner," which included many varieties of wild game, fresh vegetables, "tea & coffee & all manner of pickels with most kinds of preserves pies flavored & spiced & custards & tarts for all palates. . . ."[78] Two or three score of Ute Indians joined the diners, and soon a company of emigrants who arrived during the meal were stopped, dismounted, and placed at one of the tables, much to their surprise.[79] A company of gentlemen from Boston "appeared perfectly astonished to see the abundance and variety" of food spread out "with the greatest plenty and in taste and quantity not to be excelled."[80] And although there was no lack of enthusiasm or hilarity among the holiday crowd, "there was not a drop of strong drink anywhere to be found."[81] Brother Joseph Hovey found the whole occasion to be "a Joyful time be fore the Lorde for me."[82]

After the banquet the commemorative services started again at 3:00 P.M. with renewed vigor. There were more songs, "Yankee" stories were told, and twenty-four regular toasts, followed by volunteer toasts, some serious and some ludicrous, were made.[83] One Saint very pointedly proposed, "Martin Van Buren & all mobocrats may they be winked at by blind men kicked cross lots by cripples nibbled to death by ducks & carried to Hell through the Keyhole by Bumble Bees etc. etc. . . ."[84] The celebration ended with the crowd dispersing to their homes "and the emigrants to their wagons."[85] W. W. Call stated that it was "the most remarkable public demonstration I ever witnessed."[86]

The Pioneer Day celebration of 1850 was similar in content but lacked the spontaneous quality of the first all-out effort.[87] The parade and events were more sophisticated and included a monstrous carriage drawn by fourteen horses, references to the establishment of a university and the encouragement of home manufactures, and singing by a Welsh choir.[88] One emigrant was startled to hear much laughter at the joking opening remarks of the Prophet who said, "Between the prince of the ponies the air is kicking up a hell of dust to-day."[89] The visiting travelers were somewhat chagrined because the Mormons dispensed with a public feast "on account of pretended poverty . . . and were also very insulting to the emigrants," according to Henry Bloom.[90] John Hudson explained that the banquet was omitted due to a shortage of material that had not yet arrived in the valley from the East. Although both the Saints and the pilgrims enjoyed the spirit of the ceremonies, clearly the jubilee air of the previous year was lacking.

Of interest to many Gentile visitors were trail rumors about the hidden goings-on of polygamous families and the practice of female slavery in Salt Lake City. Some were quite circumspect in their descriptions of the very handsome Mormon ladies with their neat dress and deep sense of propriety;[91] others commented that they had never seen "so many young & beautiful girls & wives. . . ."[92] Young emigrants who stayed in the city for several weeks sometimes squired the local girls to dances and beach parties and had a glorious time, occasionally going beyond the bounds of propriety. Joseph Hamelin recorded a narrow escape in his diary when at the end of an evening of bathing in Great Salt Lake he rolled up in a blanket to sleep "although I had an invitation to sleep with a young married woman. . . ."[93] One member of a company of strangers from Cincinnati inquired of a local Mormon where he could stay through the night with some woman, and the indignant local resident replied "there were none of that kind in the City." The captain of the party was so embarrassed that he offered some stale bread to the Mormon brother.[94]

The practice of plural marriage had been surreptitiously followed during the Nauvoo period by the leadership of the Latter-day Saints. It was not openly acknowledged until a public pronouncement was made by Parley P. Pratt, at Brigham Young's direction, in Salt Lake City on August 29, 1852, the Mormon leader choosing to keep the doctrine private until the matter of a state or territorial government had been settled.[95] Many visitors, therefore, declared in letters

home or in their journals that "it is *true* that polygamy is allowed;
every man is allowed as many wives as he can or will support. . . .
Polygamy is not enjoined, but I assure you it is not prohibited."[96]
To the amazement of the travelers, they found that the Mormon men
"seem to glory in their plurality of wives," "the more women a man
can take care of here the more he is thought of."[97] William Kelly
could not believe that the spiritual wives were anything but platonic
until he discovered that they actually gave "birth to cherubs and
unfledged angels" and that there could really be two or more mistresses
in the same home.[98]

Having established that polygamy really existed, the next curiosity to be satisfied was the extent of the practice, and, specifically, the
number of wives enjoyed and supported by Brigham Young. Recent
scholarship has established that at least ten percent of the eligible
males were involved in polygamy; perhaps two-thirds of this number
had only one extra wife. Many leaders, however, had several.[99]
Franklin Langworthy heard from one Mormon elder that as many as
one-fourth of the men had at least one more wife,[100] and it was common talk among the emigrants that if the truth were known, some
Saintly leaders had as many as a dozen or more wives.[101] "One man
had 15!,"[102] with perhaps a mother-in-law attached to each wife,
according to droll William Johnston.[103] David DeWolf explained
how the process of acquiring wives worked: "Their creed allows them
a plurality of wives according to their means of supporting them &
their constitutional strength, hence a man of strong constitution &
worth much property is allowed more wives than one of weak constitution & not much of this world's goods, some of them have as high
as 40 wives."[104] It was said that the Prophet had anywhere from nineteen to sixty wives.[105] Dow Stephens tried to judge the number by the
sleeping quarters he could count at the Young residence and discovered
at least ten covered wagon bodies arranged in a row in Brigham's
backyard, each occupied by a plural wife.[106]

The adventurers would have been further amazed if they had
been privileged to hear a sermon by Heber C. Kimball in 1849 delivered to a private meeting of Saints wherein he advised the young men
in the audience to settle down and marry and build homes: "Do not
leave the young ladies to take up with strangers who will marry them.
. . ." He also counseled the middle-aged and old men to marry the girls

and treat them well since the first command was to multiply and replenish the earth. He warned, "If you do not, the time will come when you will not be permitted to do so."[107] Taking plural wives was not to be optional; it was a divine commandment.

A few excursionists were convinced that plural wives were a real economic advantage as they observed women threshing grain with flails; going into the canyons by twos or threes to gather a supply of firewood; and, of course, caring for children and households.[108] In one Mormon home, Thomas Wylly remembered seeing no teas or parties but only work inside and outside for the plural wives while the patriarch of the flock semed to eschew labor in the fields.[109] Even Brigham Young recognized the profit in plural wives, if Brother Phineas W. Cook can be believed. Cook was building a grist mill for the Prophet who brought two of his wives to the construction site to help Mrs. Cook prepare meals for the crew. Cook recorded:

> I told him that my wife was nearly tired out and we wanted to get away as soon as we could   he said he had the advantage of me for when his women got tired he would take them home and change them for fresh ones   I told him to give me time and perhaps I could do it too.   he said he was ready to give me as many as I wanted   I turned the conversation some other way as Harding was present and I did not wish to have him hear, that evening I seated myself by him alone and asked him if he meant what he said, he replied he did and he wanted me to get all the wives I wanted, and it was his council that I should do so.[110]

A survey of journals reveals that at least a few argonauts found no discord and much harmony in polygamous homes with the wives exhibiting little jealousy over their husband's attentions.[111] Gold-rusher William Black, after his conversion to Mormonism during his stopover in Salt Lake City, heeded the advice of his new leaders and married a young lady. She accepted the offer to become his second wife and agreed that he should soon return to the East to bring his first spouse and their two children back to Utah.[112]

But, perhaps understandably, most of the monogamously-oriented emigrants decried a despotic system which made a conquered people out of a lot of unhappy women who found the plurality of wives doctrine obnoxious and hateful.[113] One old sister sat in Harriet Clarke's rocking chair and with tears in her eyes told how her husband was on his way to marry as a second wife a sixteen-year-old girl. "She wanted us to take her away with us but Mr. Smith did not dare to take her."[114] This appeal to escape the cruel yoke of polygamous servitude was a common theme. Of course, there were other stories of first wives who courageously stood up to their husbands and would not allow another woman to share their spouses even though it meant "more stars in his crown of glory."[115] And polygamous husbands had their tribulations as many wives fought for their husband's favors and affections[116] or as an especially strong-minded woman "stirred up strife and contention" despite the husband's attempts to save her soul.[117]

The more hostile critics of the system could see only the strongest bestial lusts on the part of Mormon men with the marriage of a widow and several daughters, two or more sisters, or a mother and three daughters being especially repugnant.[118] There was a general view that plural marriages were of doubtful authenticity. As Hamelin opined, "If a man is dissatisfied with his bargain he can 'agree to disagree.' I have an idea of taking one on probation, say for six months, as Methodists take members into their church."[119] Once Brigham Young made the mistake of inviting a Gentile to witness him "seal a wife to Chas. W. Dollar" and was grossly insulted by the non-Mormon during the ceremony.[120] This evidence of blatant plural wifery was broadcast far and wide by the horrified emigrants during 1849, 1850, and 1851, and no doubt was an important factor in the decision to openly announce the doctrine in 1852.

Joining in the delights of a Mormon dance—the quadrille, or cotillion, or square dance, or whatever name it was called—was the chief means of recreation and social activity for the Saints and they indulged in the pastime at any opportunity. A later traveler, Richard Burton, remarked, "Dancing seems to be considered an edifying exercise. The Prophet dances, the Apostles dance, the Bishops dance."[121] Langworthy noted as he traveled through Brown's settlement near present-day Ogden that Governor Young and a large party of officials had traveled there, accompanied by the brass band, to lay out the city and, naturally held a ball in the evening. The "Pious exercise" was opened with prayer and Langworthy was not sure how proper was this "mingling of praying, fiddling, and dancing. . . ."[122] Another traveler, Dr. Edward Tompkins, who had been nursed back to health by a Mormon family, repaid his caretakers by attacking almost every aspect of Mormondom including the social dance: "They pamper the grossest senses, promote fandangos and all sorts of idle fun for the sake of making themselves believe they are happy."[123] But his was a minority report; most visiting emigrants not only approved of the dancing but were eager participants.

Some wanted the opportunity of dancing with a Mormon girl for the novelty of the thing, but most of the young men who made up the gold companies were starved for female companionship and accepted with alacrity the invitations thrust upon them to attend a ball.[124] Cotillions were held at least once a week. Jerome Howard observed the hilarity and good times associated with them and wrote, "None of the austerity of manners which usually characterizes new sects . . . is apparent among the Mormons."[125] The emigrant diaries are sprinkled with references to dance parties: "Had a good dance last night"; "Went to a dance, oyster supper, danced till daybreak"; and "The Mormons were all fond of dancing, and fortunately I was invited to several of the parties."[126] Eight of the twenty men in Hutchings' party got so carried away that they refused to leave for California at the appointed time because they had been invited to a ball that evening.[127] William Kelly attended a delightful party and was "perfectly enraptured with the Mormon ladies" and the sounds of dancing feet.[128]

Any and every occasion was used as an excuse for holding dances. There was, of course, "energetic dancing" on Pioneer Day, dancing "with great spirit" at the dedication of the Warm Springs Bath House, balls held in honor of gold companies who were departing for California, and dances at "Packs tavern," probably a private home.[129] When Brother Brigham was present, he usually led off the head of the figure.[130] A polygamous husband could encounter difficulties in trying to squire several wives around the dance floor, but Brother Wheelock was fortunate in being blessed with only three soul mates and was able to balance "first to one and then the other" as the four participated in a cotillion.[131] Edwin Hillyer enjoyed the dances he attended, and his final ecomium expressed the sentiments of many of the California-bound adventurers, "They appear to be a happy people and may they rest undisturbed."[132]

The social exchange between the emigrants and the Saints left many travelers impressed with Utah hospitality. Most eastern visitors came to admire and like their hosts although an undercurrent of bitterness over past troubles and persecutions at the hands of mid-western mobs occasionally surfaced in public statements and sermons. Specific attacks on the Presidents and other government officials were carefully recorded by some of the California-bound wayfarers and found their way into print. Later these were used to substantiate some of the charges made by the Buchanan administration.

As with any strong individual, Brigham Young aroused contro-versy, and the emigrant diaries reveal a sharp division between those who actually met him in person and liked him and his more distant auditors. Central to the dislike of Young and other Mormon leaders was the obvious evidence and open practice of polygamy. Although not yet preached from the rostrum and defended in public because there was still hope of achieving statehood, the sight of multiple wives and scores of children caused consternation ranging from bemused speculation to wrath and indignation at its abhorrent nature. Again, published emigrant diaries and letters back home began to arouse the American people to the dangers of this exotic doctrine and helped focus attention on the necessity of eradicating this evil from the fabric of society.

Socializing with the Mormons and enjoying the pleasures of bath-ing in the warm springs, attending church services and perhaps the Pioneer Day celebration, or dancing and speculating about the secret life of polygamists provided entertainment for easterners. The Saints enjoyed their visitors who brought a welcome social change. There were a few grumbles among the emigrants, but those who stopped off for a week or more usually found their hosts hospitable and full of fun. But now the party was over, and a long stretch of desert travel faced the rejuvenated gold seekers.

chapter seven

WINTER MORMONS

As the gold diggers of 1849 and 1850 looked west, they had a choice of three routes to California. The most direct was the Hastings Cutoff along the southern shores of Great Salt Lake and across a ninety-mile stretch of waterless salt flat desert to Pilot Springs near Pilot Peak. Lansford W. Hastings, a much-traveled emigrant and booster of California, published his famous *Emigrants' Guide to Oregon and California* in 1845 suggesting that this was the best road to the coast. He then learned of John C. Frémont's rather uneventful crossing of the salt flat desert in 1845 and began a campaign to publicize this shorter way to California. As a result of his promotional efforts, several emigrant companies took the route in 1846, including the ill-fated Donner Party, which suffered many hardships and delays forcing them to endure a disastrous winter in the Sierra Nevadas. During 1847, two parties of horsemen, but no wagon companies, traveled Hastings Cutoff; in 1848 only one known group of horsemen crossed on the desert trail. Captain Samuel J. Hensley attempted the route in that year but was forced to turn back. Hensley then pioneered the Salt Lake Road around the northern edge of Great Salt Lake.[1]

Despite the great rush of gold diggers through Salt Lake City in 1849, only two or three companies tried Hastings Cutoff. Part of the twenty-four-man Colony Guard outfit under Captain John McNulty traversed the "great desert of Utaria" suffering so much from thirst that they "were reduced to the necessity of drinking their mules' urine, etc. . . ."[2] The O. J. Hall manuscript mentions that a portion of his group took the trail.[3] A more descriptive and accurate account of a crossing in this year was given by Captain Stansbury who was in charge of a reconnaissance party surveying the outer rim of Great Salt Lake. He found the plain to be "as desolate, barren and dreary as can well be imagined" and during his stay in Salt Lake City warned emigrant parties to avoid it.[4]

The mad rush of impatient gold emigrants in 1850 led at least a dozen parties to use Hastings Cutoff with perhaps as many as six hundred people making the treacherous crossing. Determined to take the shortest route, they disregarded information about safer routes and agreed with Finley McDiarmid to try Hastings Cutoff, "The advice of Capt Stansbury and all the Mormons to the contrary notwithstanding."[5] Among those who left records of traveling the trail in this year were Silas Newcomb; John Udell; Robert Chalmers; one single group of about three hundred under the leadership of Auguste Archambault, Frémont's guide; Madison Moorman; Henry Bloom; John Wood; John L. Brown; David Hobson; and John R. Shinn. All described the extreme suffering of men and animals as water gave out and the insufficient supplies of cut grass disappeared. Soon the exhausted animals dropped in their tracks. Men on foot pushed on to Pilot Springs and then returned with life-saving water for those too weak to continue.[6] John B. McGee wrote the editor of the *Deseret News* on July 29, 1850, warning that travelers *"can not* get through with their animals without at *least 2 gallons* of *water* to *each animal and* one gallon for each person," plus a supply of grass for the stock. Joseph Cain's letter to the *Deseret News* of October 5, 1850, indicated that the road was much longer and more dangerous than advertised. The salt desert trail was not used after 1850, and the only reminders of Hastings Cutoff are the relics of wagons still evident a hundred years later.

The more careful travelers and by far the largest number of emigrant trains chose to proceed along the Salt Lake Road north from Salt Lake City past the present towns of Bountiful, Hooper, Plain City, Willard, Brigham City, to Collinston and the crossing of Bear River, to a point just west of Plymouth through Rocky Ford of the Malad River, west past Snowville, and then through Emigration Canyon to a junction with the Fort Hall Road just south of City of Rocks. When Captain Samuel J. Hensley opened this main route in August 1848, he led a party of ten men on horseback along the road from Salt Lake City to the ford at Bear River eighty miles to the north. On August 27, Hensley was on the Humboldt River where he met a group of men who had been discharged from the Mormon Battalion traveling to

Salt Lake Valley. On the advice of the captain, the former soldiers decided to take their large party of 45 men and one woman, 17 wagons, and 150 horses along Hensley's new trail instead of going by the longer Fort Hall route. They thus took the first wagons over the Salt Lake Road and marked it for the thousands of forty-niners and 1850 migrants who chose this passage.[7]

As the gold-rushers left the oasis of civilization at Salt Lake City behind, they found a few more opportunities at Brownsville or the Ogden settlement, about forty miles to the north, to trade jaded cattle for fresh ones or to get a last home-cooked meal for $.50.[8] By the summer of 1850 there were eight houses and a blacksmith shop at Brownsville and ten log cabins at Ogden.[9] McKeeby noted that at the last house, fifty miles from Salt Lake City, there was a family composed of an old retired army officer and his two young wives who "apparently like their position of joint wifehood."[10]

The emigrants had to cross three streams on the Salt Lake Road where ferries run by Mormons were operated on a hit-or-miss basis. At the first, Weber River, the operator charged anywhere from $.50 for ferrying baggage across the stream[11] to $3.00 for a wagon. Horses and mules had to swim the swift current, which could be very dangerous at flood tide. At the smaller Ogden River, the price for a wagon was only $2.[12] Early in 1850 some enterprising Mormons built rickety bridges over the two rivers but, as the *Deseret News* of June 22, 1850, described it, they "sailed down stream the first spring freshet. . . ."

At Bear River, a dangerous, terrible stream,[13] the traffic was heavy as the ferry operators and their "scift"[14] (three canoes with planks tied on with rawhide and "a very poor sort of a concern to risk our waggon"[15]) attempted to meet the demand. Cautious travelers sometimes persuaded the ferryman at the Weber River to haul his craft up to "Bare" river so they would be sure of crossing.[16] The charges ranged from $.25 per man to $2.00 per wagon, and to as high as $7.00 at the height of the rush.[17] Nelson Slater accused the Mormon leaders of encouraging the overlanders to travel the Salt Lake Road in order to make a profit off ferriage, which he claimed was as high as $8.00 for a wagon and team.[18] Samuel Dundass complained of the "extortion, man's inhumanity to man . . . a most exorbitant price" levied by the ferrymen,[19] and when Simon Doyle's party reached the stream, they refused to pay the modest price of $5.00 per wagon, started digging out the banks to make a ford, and finally forced the operators to agree to ferry them across at $.50 per wagon plus one yoke of oxen.[20] This was on July 27. By mid-August, the river was so low that the ferry ceased operations for that year.[21]

A few miles from Bear River the travelers encountered one more narrow stream, the Malad. Apparently they had to cross it any way they could during the first gold rush year, sometimes wading in water up to their chins.[22] By 1850 a Mormon Brother was charging $1.00 per wagon to travel over his "very rough & shackling bridge."[23] Beyond the Malad there was only desert and the emigrants were out of Mormon country.

The gold hunters of 1849 who arrived too late to take either the Hastings or the Salt Lake roads had the choice of remaining in the City of the Saints over the winter or taking the southern route by the Old Spanish Trail to Los Angeles. Some cautious souls, as early as August, made the decision to wait for cool weather and the southern tour, believing the rumors that Indians had burned the grass along the Humboldt Trail[24] which was "so obstructed with dead cattle as to admit no passage for waggons."[25] It was also reported that some starving emigrant parties had run into snow in the Sierras and had had to return to Salt Lake Valley;[26] and that the Mormon leaders, fearing that "so large an accession of mouths, in addition to those of our own emigration, threatened almost a famine for bread," were pronouncing travel by the northern road this late to be "madness"[27] and so encouraged the late season travelers to take the southern route.[28] The approximately 750 adventurers who chose to go by way of the Old Spanish Trail in 1849 were so anxious to reach California before all the nuggets had been gathered that they did not heed any advice from their Mormon hosts—they just hurried on to the mines as fast as they could.

The largest of the six organized companies was led by Jefferson Hunt, a Mormon who had been over the trail in 1847-48 and who offered to guide a party of emigrants for the sum of ten dollars per wagon. Eventually the owners of about 100 wagons signed up and gathered at Fort Utah, forty miles south of Salt Lake City, to organize their "Sand Walking Company" (from San Joaquin), to recruit their stock, and to trade for horses with the neighboring Ute Indians. While awaiting cooler weather, the emigrants enjoyed the hospitality of

Mormon settlers and participated in a "blow-out" celebration held in honor of a visit from Brigham Young. They also prepared for the arduous trip which finally started in early October.[29]

After several days of travel, one of the emigrant packers, O. K. Smith, consulted a map he had obtained showing a shortcut which would supposedly save twenty days and 500 miles. Despite Captain Hunt's strong objections, all but seven of the wagons went with Smith. But after encountering some very difficult terrain, over 300 of the people returned to the Old Spanish Trail and followed Hunt who was by now seven days ahead. Hunt and his rear guard finally reached California at Christmastime. The remaining Smith converts struggled along on "Walker's Cutoff" suffering terribly, losing some members in death, and with a few crossing the stretch of desert which has since borne the name Death Valley.[30]

Other smaller parties of 1849 included the Gruwell-Duer company of twenty-three wagons under a Mexican guide, which left in advance of the Hunt expedition and reached California in two segments by late December and early January.[31] The Pomeroy company, a group led by Howard Egan, and one under S. D. Huffaker,[32] kept to the known trail and arrived in California in early 1850. There were about 100 emigrants in these companies. Even though they encountered the troubles usually associated with traveling through a water-parched terrain, most arrived safely and in good time—a few in as little as fifty days. The approximately 100 followers of O. K. Smith eventually split up into at least ten known groups with the longest-suffering component, the Death Valley contingent, taking a full four months to travel over the twenty-day route.[33]

The 1850 emigrants traveling the southwest trail had safer journeys. A Mormon, mountaineer, Barney Ward, offered to guide a train to Los Angeles for ten dollars a wagon but at the last minute withdrew from his contract. Several hundred emigrants traveled the road, with or without guides, certain that they did not want to share the fate of the Donner Party by tackling the Sierra Nevadas late in the season. The Ward company composed of ninety wagons set out without precise information about the route, although they may have purchased a way bill of the road which was advertised for sale by Joseph Cain in the *Deseret News* on October 5, 1850, just three days before they left Salt Lake City. The newspaper had already certified on September 7

and 14 that the Old Spanish Trail was "a good road" which was safe
and "far pleasanter than the Northern Route." The ninety-wagon
company reached the Los Angeles area in two and a half months,
a typical schedule for the 1850 emigrants.[34]

Travel by both the southern route and Hastings Cutoff involved
only about ten percent of the more than 10,000 overlanders of 1849
and perhaps a like percentage of the approximately 15,000 travelers
for 1850 who chose to go through Salt Lake City. The Salt Lake Road
was a well-marked thoroughfare for the main body of the gold-rushers.

A few ill, impecunious, or tired out pilgrims stayed behind to
spend the winter; other travelers decided to join the Mormon church.
Latter-day Saint missionaries looked upon the gold rush migration as
an unparalleled opportunity to preach their gospel message. As Parley
P. Pratt explained, "Great numbers of strangers attend our meetings
now every Sabbath, and we feel as if we were about in the middle of
the world, and in as good a place to preach the gospel to all the world
as can be found."[35] Furthermore, local elders were assigned by their
bishops to do team proselyting among the strangers. William Wilson,
recorded, "We expect a Mormon preching tonite in our camps."[36]
Individual Mormons, in their private conversations with travelers or
while engaged in trading, also used every chance to explain "the
principles of the doctrine of Christ in their purity."[37]

Overlanders explained the Mormons' success in converting visitors variously, but one of the foremost reasons given was "their many
deeds of charity to the sick and broken-down gold-seekers. . . ."[38]
Charles Smith had been injured when he became entangled in a rope.
He decided to spend the winter in Salt Lake City recuperating and
eventually joined the Mormon church.[39] One man was converted
because some elders had cured his dying brother by the "laying on of
hands."[40] John Hudson, after being restored to health in the Mormon
city, wrote his family in Birmingham, England, about how inspiring
it was to "hear the glorious gospel [and] live under a pure administration of just and sacred law. . . ."[41] Hudson joined the church but
was apparently too embarrassed to tell his family, which only learned
of his conversion following his death on December 14, 1850, in Sanpete Valley where he had gone as a colonizer on a "call" from Brigham
Young.[42]

Langworthy made a scientific appraisal of the reasons for Mormon success: (1) their theology could be stretched to become all things to all men, (2) they promised great temporal benefits in free land in the American Eden to poor people in Europe, (3) to the wealthy, the Mormons held out the promise of high church office, the opportunity for financial advancement, and, not least, "Seraglios" filled with women, (4) the persecutions in Illinois and Missouri excited the sympathy of some, and (5) a secret, mystic order resembling Free Masonry offered advantages.[43]

Church writers tended to exaggerate the number of converts from among the argonauts: "Many scores, if not hundreds . . . hearing the gospel . . . have been baptized." A more conservative observer merely noted "a few of them embraced the Gospel. . . ."[44] Mormon leaders took pride each Sabbath in announcing in meeting the names of emigrants who had united with the Saints during the previous week.[45] Most converts elected to give up their quest for gold although a few continued on. Albert Thurber had stepped out of his tent pitched in the old Fort and asked, " 'What kind of a God do you Mormons believe in?' and a young man answered, 'We believe in a God with body, parts, and passions, one that can see, hear, talk and walk.' " Thurber was satisfied with the answer and joined the church shortly after. But he went on to the California gold fields, where he spent several months before returning to Utah. He later became the mayor of Spanish Fork.[47]

William Black converted after listening to testimonies given in the Bowery. Black asked for baptism immediately after the meeting but was counselled by William Wordsworth to study the doctrine first. He remained faithful to his new convictions and was finally accepted into the church even though parting from friends in his gold rush company was painful.[48] Not all new members were as carefully nurtured in the theology before being baptized. Gunnison met a young man from Michigan who had joined the Mormon faith but had spent his time in Salt Lake City reading novels instead of the Book of Mormon. The army officer thought "such blind going to work on immortal subjects is surprising."[49]

Not all missionary activity was successful. A few of the excursionists feigned interest in the Mormon faith in order to get the supplies they needed to continue their journey. One young man professed much concern about learning the truth from his bishop host while the women of the household "were loading the table with good things. . . ." Afterwards he enjoined his comrades to silence while they continued the charade.[50] Perhaps it was understandable that some Mormon preachers, meeting such subtle opposition or outright hostility, "stamped the dust" off their feet before giving up their proselyting efforts.[51]

Recruiting new members was actively pursued by the Mormon women, one of whom, an old lady from Vermont, "tried hard to convert" John Carr assuring him he would become "a splendid Mormon." She was unsuccessful.[52] Several ladies gave Edwin Hillyer a strong invitation to join the church but he also declined.[53]

There were many overlanders, of course, who did not join the church but who chose to return to Salt Lake City for the winter because of Indian attacks[54] or lack of grass along the Humboldt.[55] Others arrived so late that even the possibility of traveling the southwest trail to Los Angeles seemed out of the question. A party from Michigan reached Salt Lake City on November 15, 1849, and found two inches of snow on the valley floor.[56] A later company of nineteen men came in on December 1, "in a very destitute situation" having left their wagons forty miles back and their teams about twenty miles away where the snow was six feet deep on the level.[57] Early exaggerated reports indicated that perhaps as many as 15,000 emigrants would be forced to winter at Salt Lake City in 1849, but only 3,000 stayed with most eventually traveling on to southern California.[58] According to some adventurers, the reason for not remaining among the Mormons through the winter was "mainly owing to the uncongeniality of feeling" between the Gentiles and the residents.[59] But most moved on because they feared the gold would be gone if they did not hurry.[60]

Of the gold-rushers who remained behind in 1849 and 1850, a few converted while seeking winter employment and enjoying the cultural pursuits of the valley and while making preparations to continue their journey.[61] Hosea Stout explained the difference between these new members who married Mormon girls and the gold-rushers who remained Gentiles: "Winter saints are those Emegrants who stop here, join the church & marry wives and go to the mines in the Spring etc." Winter Mormons, on the other hand, were the non-joiners among the Gentile emigrants who merely stopped off awaiting the coming of spring.[62]

John Hudson joined the church but did not marry and still intended to travel on to the gold fields. He described his 1849–50 job as a school teacher at the frontier post of Fort Utah.

> You will like to know how I succeeded in the capacity of School-master, it is true that I had more to contend with than I anticipated, the children, from rude habits acquired on the road to the valley, & the few educational privileges they have enjoyed, were at first a little unmanageable,—the mild measures I at first adopted, were forced to be changed for those a little more peremptory, & then with the cooperation of their Parents my rule was established & these difficulties ceased; I had about 30 boys & girls none of whom studied anything more scientific than arithmetic, so I jogged along pretty easily, & was popular both with pupils & parents. Could you but have seen my school, it would have appeared both novel & interesting a rude log cabin 16 ft. square daubed with mud to exclude the cold air, with no flooring save that afforded by mother earth then my furniture consisted in a bedstead which stood in one corner, & as it was made by myself you may judge how little elegance entered into its composition; this not only served as a couch by night, but as during school hours an elevated seat from which I could survey my charges.[63]

Not all the Winter Saints were impelled by pure motives when they entered into matrimony with local girls. Permission to wed was usually dependent on membership in the church and parents abhorred the thought of their daughters marrying outside the Mormon covenant.[64] A few years later, Frederick Kesler expressed his bitter disappointment when two of his daughters married nonmembers: "2 of my Daughters Have been led away by the eavil influances of the Jentiles it makes me feel like Girding on my armour and going forth and laying waste these poor miserable Curses that Have Run the cause of leading astray 2 of my Daughters. . . ."[65]

After the first winter's experience, and with a new season approaching Elder Orson Hyde felt the problem of Winter Saints was so serious that he addressed a letter, "Advice to Females," to the *Deseret News* on October 5, 1850. He welcomed converts from among the emigrants as long as they came with honest hearts and sincere convictions, but he counseled female readers to be on guard against "transient and uncertain" travelers who might have families in the states. He thought that as many as four out of five of the eastern nomads who sought marriage were serpents in the grass, hypocrites, and unprincipled men whose advances the women of Mormondom should carefully examine before allowing these false-hearted libertines "to gain a seat in their affections. . . ."

Brother Hyde was not just whistling in the wind. Two California-bound German emigrants who married Mormon girls set up a butcher shop in the city but were soon caught stealing an ox and were accused of other thefts. In the first jury trial under the laws of the new State of Deseret, they were convicted and sentenced to $200 fines or two years at hard labor.[66] They may have suffered the fate of other kindred spirits. Hosea Stout reported on January 19, 1851, "In the after noon went to meeting again. Some 6 or 8 of the *Winter Saints* and their wives were cut off from the Church."[67]

Among the Gentile emigrants who wintered in Salt Lake, a few departed in the spring of 1851 determined to publish to the world the supposed wrongs they had suffered. While only a few hundred had stopped over in 1849–50, during the next winter almost 900 remained in Salt Lake City, and their accusations were soon broadcast by the nation's press, both in the West and in the East. This litany of charges eventually culminated in the Utah War between the Mormons and the James Buchanan government in 1857. The 1851 confrontation, as recorded in emigrant memorials and newspaper indictments, was one-sided because the Mormons did not comment and did not have access to many newspapers. The Winter Mormons were certainly in a less than favorable economic bargaining position with their hosts and also, just as irritating, were subjected to Mormon law and court processes, which some thought unfair and wholly un-American.

There were three principal reporters of alleged Mormon wrong-doings, two of whom spent the 1850–51 winter in Salt Lake Valley. Franklin Langworthy, the Universalist preacher who had been given the privilege of speaking in the Bowery on August 11, 1850,[68] was hostile from the beginning. In 1855, five years after reaching the coast, he published his diary along with an extensive analysis of what he considered subversive activities against the government. He also included an attack on Mormon theology.[69] Of more importance were Nelson Slater and the Reverend J. W. Goodell who spent the winter of 1850–51 at Salt Lake. Slater's book, *Fruits of Mormonism*, published in 1851, became the basis for many newspaper articles explaining the secrets of Mormondom hidden away in the Wasatch Mountains.[70] In the winter of 1851 the Reverend Goodell and other emigrants finally moved to Willow Creek sixty miles north of Salt Lake City in a defiant attempt to escape Mormon control. He wrote nine letters to the *Portland Weekly Oregonian* in the spring of 1852 in which he acted as spokesman for his fellow adventurers and related the apparent wrongs they had endured while in Salt Lake Valley.[71]

In an attempt to counter questions about their objectivity, Slater, Goodell, and Langworthy explained that the Mormons were quite open, friendly, and fair in their dealings with summer travelers, but once the unsuspecting had committed themselves to a winter sojourn, their hosts at once assailed them. The emigrants claimed Mormon leaders had encouraged them to remain in order to get trained artisans for various projects at reduced wages, to raise money through a personal tax imposed on visitors, to increase Utah's population to improve the possibility of gaining statehood for Deseret, and to provide a reservoir from among whom souls might be saved. Individual Saints might have been motivated in these ways, but it is unlikely that Mormon leaders deliberately schemed to effect these ends, although they were not reluctant to accept the benefits that resulted.

The triumvirate of accusers generally complained about economic exploitation. The greatest concern was the two percent personal property tax assessed all residents which the emigrants thought was "illegal and arbitrary."[72] What was worse, according to Slater, was that the visitors were not aware they would have to pay this tax until the end of their winter's stay. Solomon Zumwalt was levied a tax of $19.80;[73] Goodell paid $18.80 on two wagons, four yoke of oxen, four cows, and some personal effects. A man from Missouri with five wagons was forced to pay a $60 tax. If a temporary resident could not pay in cash, sometimes the sheriff would possess his team and wagon and deprive him of the means of escaping from Mormon territory unless friends would come to his rescue, according to Slater and Goodell.[74]

At first Mormon employers treated their emigrant laborers fairly but supposedly as soon as the first snow fell, wages were reduced or paid in produce. Instructions came from on high to withhold all cash from the overlanders so usually they left the valley poorer than when they entered. Slater claimed the church leadership employed men to steal emigrant stock or to run it off to distant herd grounds. If a Gentile tried to recover his property in court, he found himself paying $6.00 to have a summons issued, $6.00 for a constable to serve it, and $1.50 per mile for travel charges.[75] Above all, travelers were advised to have no "business transactions" with Apostle Ezra T. Benson who was the chief extorter of all the Mormon leaders, if Slater were to be believed.[76]

Not only did the Saints take financial advantage of their Gentile employees but they were remorseless toward sick people left in their care. In one instance, according to Slater, a Mormon family appropriated all of their patient's property worth $150 and, in a second case, another host charged an invalid $138 which he was forced to pay before being allowed to leave.[77] Even the dead received scant attention. An emigrant was killed by Indians near Ogden, but the local residents there would not prepare a coffin for him, failed to furnish enough men to carry the coffin to the grave, and refused to hold a funeral service—"it was more like the burial of an ass than that of a human being."[78] The practice of taking control of the estates of deceased individuals was common in Salt Lake City, including in one case confiscation of the dental instruments of a doctor. This, again, was from Slater.[79]

A minor irritant for many of the adventurers of 1850 was the anti-swearing law passed in February 1851 after Brigham Young had preached "against swearing & other profane and such like immoral practices."[80] In fact, Brigham went beyond this and advised the officers of the law to report oath-takers who should then be cut off the church and he added that "if any of his boys were heard swearing, any one that did not swear was at liberty to knock them down or horse whip them. . . ."[81] Goodell thought it was like "the devil punishing sin" because he didn't observe any Saints being arrested for violating the law although many of them cursed the "damned Missourians."[82] The Gentiles suffered, some being sentenced to the public works under ball and chain or at least fined five dollars and costs. S. M. Bowman, Esq., warned others not to stop in Salt Lake City if they were at all profane.[83] John Verdenal wrote that by 1852 the authorities were prohibiting "the use of liquors, and smoking or chewing tobacco" as well as swearing.[84] And yet the winter Mormons were accommodated with grog shops which sold a local whiskey at six dollars a gallon, a "valley tan" rum made of molasses and green tea for eight dollars a gallon, and a light beer described as wholesome.[85]

All three publicists accused the Mormons of instituting "nuisance lawsuits" which the emigrants always lost because they had to pay outrageously high court costs. Goodell was especially indignant over the theft of three bushels of his wheat by a Mormon. The thief paid for the stolen goods, but just as Goodell was preparing to leave the territory, the unrepentant Saint took him to court demanding the return of the money. After three trials, a "no cause for action" decision was rendered by the judge but, to the amazement and anger of Goodell, the justice assessed him $75.00 for court costs.[86] Slater listed nine cases involving emigrants which were "a mere farce," and "a mockery of justice." One had to do with a hen found dead near an easterner's camp for which the emigrant was fined $10.00 damages and $8.00 costs although a chicken was worth only $.50 at the time.[87] The disgruntled adventurers were certain that it was impossible to get impartial justice when a Mormon was the adversary.

Verbal abuse of the national government and subversive talk and unpatriotic actions by Mormon leaders could not be tolerated any longer according to Slater, Goodell, Langworthy, and some less articulate overlanders. These shocked listeners heard church authorities denounce the government as an enemy, state that the government should be overthrown, that military supplies were being collected for a possible war with the United States, and that Mormon and Gentile alike lived under a "despotism" in Utah. The church leadership was also charged with inciting Indians to murder "Americans," opening United States mail, and infringing on other personal liberties.[88] Brigham Young and his colleagues were accused of harboring the vicious "Danites" who were used as spies and to kill the enemies of the church. Supposedly Brigham's faithful followers were taught that "a person cannot be a mormon without having a gun, nor can he have religion without knowing how to use it," but they also were afraid to speak out against the prophet.[89]

Of all the alleged Mormon atrocities, the killing of Dr. John M. Vaughn received the greatest publicity. A report of this incident was made to the President of the United States on December 19, 1851, by three of Utah Territory's disgruntled officials—Chief Justice

Lemuel G. Brandenbury, Associate Justice Perry E. Brocchus, and Secretary B. D. Harris.[90] Slater, Goodell, and Langworthy all reported it and it became a national cause célèbre.[91]

Not much is known about John M. Vaughn. The earliest notice of his medical practice in Salt Lake City appears in Leonard E. Harrington's journal: "I had the misfortune to fall and break my arm, which was very badly set by Dr. Vaughn and was nearly useless for the whole winter."[92] Despite this poor reference, apparently Vaughn held a position of some respect. Midwife Patty Sessions noted on July 31, 1850, "I then went to the Medical Meeting; Saw a Doctor Vaun heard him and Dr. Benson talk."[93] Vaughn ran an advertisement in the *Deseret News* during July and August of 1850 which explained that although he was a graduate of the "Old School," he was not committed to any special kind of medicine and was ready to accept any part of the art which would help in healing people. His office was posted as being at the house of Timothy B. Foote, near the Bath House.[94] In September 1850 Vaughn was charged by Foote with having committed adultery with Mrs. Foote. The case ended when Governor Young released Doctor Vaughn on the grounds that Foote had failed to sustain the charge of immoral conduct.[95] Vaughn at once decided to leave Salt Lake City and went with the young Englishman, John Hudson, to Manti in Sanpete Valley in central Utah. However, Vaughn soon demonstrated that he had not profited from his experience.[96]

By February 1851 he was having an affair with Chelnicio Hambleton, the wife of Madison D. Hambleton of Manti, and the mother of two daughters. Azariah Smith, also a resident of Manti, recorded the outcome of the liaison between Vaughn and Mrs. Hambleton:

> Thursday February the 6th [1851] Last Sunday . . . after the meeting was dismissed I started for home, but after geting about 20.foot from the door I stoped to look around and just as I looked around I heard the report of a pistol shot about four foot from me, which was loaded very heavy; I instantly looked around and saw brother Hamilton just taking his pistol from his face, having shot doctor Vaughn through his left arm, and in to his body, and it is supposed that the boll struck his heart. . . . [he] did not live but a short time. Brother Hamilton had been up north to work, and while he was gone, this doctor Vaughn had been keeping company considerable

with his wife, and it was proven that one night as she was undressing herself to go to bed; (there being a young man and woman in the room at the time), the doctor came in; Mrs. Hamilton immediately dressed herself again and seting down by the side of the doctor they played and joked together awhile when the doctor blew out the candle and then covered up all of the fire. they then went back in the back part of the room, and stayed for some time. They then came back to the fire lighting the candle: and the young man that was there says that he told doctor Vaughn at the time that Hamilton would shoot him, but he said that old folks knew more than young ones. there was other instances of the same kind proven against him and it was hinted to him by several that if he did not change himself that he would get shot, but after Hamilton came home the doctor every chance that he could get he would slip in with Mrs. Hamilton; and she has been a mean character for some time. And Hamilton being somewhat mad, on Sunday after meting shot down the doctor; and he said that the children was all that saved his wife.[97]

Hambleton surrendered himself to his bishop and was sent to Salt Lake City for trial where the Supreme Court of the Territory heard the case. Governor Brigham Young represented Hambleton and Hosea Stout spoke for Deseret in a Court of Inquiry, not a criminal trial. The governor's speech in justification of Hambleton's action cleared him of any wrongdoing. Stout concluded that Vaughn's "seduction & illicit conversation with Mrs. Hambleton was sufficiently proven insomuch that I was well satisfied of his justification as well as all who were present and plead to the case to that effect. He was acquitted by the Court and also by the Voice of the people present."[98]

The evidence against Vaughn was certainly circumstantial. The other charges by the emigrant polemicists were likewise correct—Hambleton was never arrested, there was no criminal trial, and the Governor of Deseret represented him, quite an unusual procedure. The resolution of the Vaughn case redounded to the discredit of the Saints, although it was perhaps understandable under the standards of the time and Vaughn's disreputable character.

The various accusations levied against the Mormon people were founded in an abhorrence of polygamy shared by Goodell and Langworthy, both ministers of the gospel, and by Slater, a schoolteacher. The Latter-day Saints, according to their critics, disregarded the Bible, made little pretense of keeping the Sabbath day holy, and actually held dancing parties in new churches which were being dedicated.

But these were minor religious infractions compared to the "open, unblushing, beastly impurity and vileness" of the practice of plural marriage. As the Reverend Goodell explained to the editor of the *Oregonian*, if he dared to tell all of the shameful things he knew about spiritual wifery, the newspaperman would not publish it—it was "too polluting" to record. Goodell reported that the prophet had 70 or 80 wives and was continually adding to the number. Slater reported that there were nine children born in one day to Brigham's wives and that one of his counselors, probably Heber C. Kimball, had eighteen children so young none had learned to walk. The plural wives were involved in a real slave system from which they could not escape. The shocked emigrant reporters called upon the people and government of the United States to eradicate the cancer of polygamy from the body politic. The practice of "concubinage" by the Mormons of Utah was very likely a root cause of the virulent attacks mounted against them by Winter Mormons.[99]

"Cabin fever" at the foot of the Wasatch Mountains affected both Gentiles and Saints and exacerbated differences only lightly felt during the short summer stopovers. The two percent tax ground on the nerves of Winter Mormons. And just as some emigrants assailed Mormon leaders while forgiving deluded followers, Brigham Young and his authorities condemned national politicians while professing loyalty and faith in the Constitution and the United States government.

Latter-day Saint excoriations of the Winter Mormons were few. As indicated earlier, the *Deseret News* of March 22, 1851, complained about California emigrants who dumped their sick on the Salt Lake residents and also condemned careless travelers who allowed their stock to break into fields. With these exceptions, few charges were made against the wintering gold seekers.

Interactions between individual Saints and Gentiles could result in trouble. When the son of Winter Mormon Solomon Zumwalt and another boy "bore down hard on the Mormons" to a group that included some Saints, they were reported to city authorities who threatened to run off Zumwalt's cattle. After Zumwalt had gone to explain to Mormon leaders that he held no ill will toward them, "they made light of it, said there were as bad people in the Mormon Church as there were anywhere. So I was all right again."[100] Some difficulties between the two groups stemmed from intransigence and downright orneriness resulting from the breakdown of communication common to peoples of different religious persuasions and political backgrounds.

The impressions the departing emigrants had of Salt Lake City and its inhabitants depended, of course, upon individual experiences. Winter Saints, leaving for California with Mormon wives, or, more likely, leaving their new spouses behind, might well have contemplated an enjoyable winter spent in the valley. A few Winter Mormons, on the other hand, hurried away from the theocracy and tight control of Brigham Young and his fellow leaders and found the first opportunity to tell the world about the discrimination suffered. But most of the travelers could remember a pleasant stopover at the City of the Saints where supplies and new stock enabled them to pursue their golden dream.

History has tended to downplay the latter, perhaps because satisfied customers fail to publicize their good fortune and kind treatment, while the discontented or malevolent tend to seek every means to advertise their negative feelings. Certainly Slater and Goodell were heard by eastern America almost immediately after their arrival on the Pacific Coast. These two and Langworthy caught the attention of those in Washington, D.C., and elsewhere, who were now confirmed in their suspicions and distrust of the Mormons.

The two-year rush of gold seekers left a heritage of friendship and good feelings between the Saints and the majority of visitors. It was unfortunate that a few discordant notes would sour the improving relationship between the nation and the persecuted Mormon people.

chapter eight

END OF THE GOLDEN RAINBOW

THE gold-rushers of 1849 and 1850 were well named. Their motivation was to get to California, to get rich, and to get back home to the states and civilization. Their companies were made up almost exclusively of males; only about two percent of the travelers were women.[1] They were in a hurry; they started out heavily laden, but many discarded their wagons and packed through the last 700 miles. The elephant they found in California was a huge disappointment for most, and when this news filtered back East, the gold mania ended as abruptly as it started. Newspapers and journals in the spring of 1851 heralded the change which prompted many to reverse their course and become "back out Gold diggers."[2] The cold statistics revealed the dramatic shift: 25,450 people to the West Coast in 1849; 50,000 in 1850; and only 4,700 in 1851. When westward travel began again in 1852 with 60,000 traversing the trail to California and Oregon, it was a different kind of emigration.[3]

Mormon newspapers chronicled the new character of these later western travelers. Most of them called themselves "Oregon emigrants" with a few opining that they might go south to California later to see if there was any gold left. These were families, accompanied by cows, sheep, and other stock—evidence that the new emigrants were looking for permanent homes.[4] The *Frontier Guardian* was pleased because they would be "certain to make the Wilderness bud, and blossom as the rose, and the solitary place glad."[5] At least one large sheep herd went through Salt Lake Valley in 1851 en route for California, another sign of stability for that volatile land.[6]

Before there was much indication that the 1851 emigration would be reduced to one-fifth of what it was the previous year, the Mormon leaders strongly expressed the hope that travelers would go by way of Fort Hall or another route.[7] The few emigrants who did head for Oregon this year tended to take their chances on getting through to the coast or stocking up at trading posts on the way instead of stopping off at Salt Lake City.[8] As a result there were few ads for emigrant services in the *Deseret News,* and both Mormons and Gentiles seemed pleased that there was little necessity of traveling through Mormondom. Merchants who had depended on emigrant trade for extra profits suffered somewhat, and everyone in the valley noted the scarcity of money.[9] The gold rush had ended.

Throughout the two years of travel by way of the Mormon Halfway House, the Latter-day Saints and their Gentile visitors shared a sometimes uneasy but on the whole comfortable relationship. The tribulations and persecutions suffered by the Mormons in Missouri and Illinois were still fresh, and the memories of the loss of loved ones at the camps in Iowa and along the trail to the Great Basin still rankled. It was amazing that the incoming emigrants did not sometimes meet greater hostility. The counsel of Brigham Young and other leaders to practice Christian brotherhood, and the economic benefits brought by the adventurers, tended to soften resentment or recrimination. The emigrants were so caught up in gold fever and were so desperate for provisions and fresh animals that they, too, were accommodating. For most of them this was their first experience with Mormons and curiosity helped develop a good relationship. Some pilgrims came with prejudice and retained their bias just as some Saints could not forget wrongs visited upon them by Gentiles.

After initial contacts with Mormon ferrymen and trading families along the Overland Trail, the argonauts descended into Salt Lake City to feast on green garden vegetables, to divide their company stores in preparation for the final trek, and to hear Mormon fulminations against gold grabbing. Salt Lake City soon turned into a giant supermarket as the Saints crowded around the newcomers' wagon boxes to buy scarce supplies and drive shrewd bargains as travelers traded off worn-out and exhausted oxen, mules, and horses for fresh animals. Early entrepreneurs set up shop to share in the bonanza created by the gold-rushers' desire for goods. For the Saints, the coming of thousands of easterners with manufactured articles, clothing, and groceries seemed miraculous and their starvation period during the winter of 1848–49 was soon forgotten as abundance poured upon them.

Occasionally there were irritations for both sides. Sharp trading practices by some Saints caused resentment; emigrant arguments over division of property led to court litigation and tiresome quarreling which upset the tranquility of the valley. Some of the laws of Deseret seemed ludicrous and harsh to excursionists, especially if they happened to get caught in the toils of the law. The Mormon justices of the peace administered their decisions with impartiality and common sense, which most emigrants accepted with equanimity or at least resignation.

The social relationships between Mormon and Gentile were mostly friendly, especially if the visitors tarried in Salt Lake City. The tired emigrants enjoyed bathing in the warm springs, visiting Mormon church services in the Bowery, celebrating Pioneer Day, and speculating on how many wives Brigham Young had as they discussed the strange practice of polygamy and attended Mormon dancing parties. The Saints entered into the excitement and novelty of the thousands of visitors camping around and in their city and visiting them in their homes.

A more somber note was introduced during the winter of 1850 when almost 900 emigrants, now Winter Mormons, settled down for the cold season in Salt Lake Valley. Some had joined the Mormon church and were soon absorbed into their new-found faith; many others found jobs and settled into a comfortable and friendly routine with their hosts; a few found their stay in Mormondom irksome or even dangerous if the charges of people like Slater and Goodell were true. A significant result of the accusations against the Mormons leveled by hostile critics was to start a storm of protest against alleged Mormon disloyalty which culminated in the federal army being sent against the Saints in 1857. But for the 25,000 travelers who had already passed through Salt Lake City, their stay had been friendly and profitable. When the summer of 1851 revealed only a few emigrant wagons meandering through the Golden Pass to Salt Lake City, the Saints again accepted isolation. Another year passed before a flood of visitors of a different sort came into the valley; this time they were families and homeseekers on their way to farms in Oregon and California. The Far West settled down to the more gradual development that had characterized the early frontier.

The two-year rush of emigration through Salt Lake City did have some far-reaching effects. One obvious result was a change in travel patterns for those seekings homes or fortunes on the Pacific slope. The Hastings Cutoff south of Great Salt Lake was discredited and declared unsafe; the Salt Lake Road north of the lake was established as the most practical way to reach the California Trail from the Utah settlements. Later, as the Union Pacific and Central Pacific railroads contemplated the easiest and most direct route through Utah Territory, they chose to follow this path, much to the chagrin of Brigham Young who wanted the new railroad to pass through Salt Lake City. The southern route to Los Angeles also became well known to many outside the Great Basin because of the large gold-rush parties who traveled the road in 1849 and 1850. And Parley P. Pratt's new Golden Pass Road east through the Wasatch Mountains soon led to the abandonment of the tortuous travel through Emigration Canyon. Today's automobiles take this route through Parleys Canyon following Interstate 80 on six lanes of concrete carved out of the rocky chasm.

Although the myth of the "Great American Desert" covering the Great Plains and extending through the Great Basin had already been suggested to the American people, it became a fixed idea as the gold emigrants, used to the well-watered East and Midwest, reported their sufferings to the folks back home. They did marvel at the green oasis nurtured in this desert by the intrepid Mormons and were much intrigued by the system of irrigation devised to water farms and gardens, perhaps the first time this experiment was widely publicized to eastern readers. Emigrant diaries and letters also provided the first accurate knowledge to many Americans of Salt Lake City and its Mormon inhabitants. Later investigators like Sir Richard Burton and lesser reporters like William Chandless in the 1850s could well have been influenced in their desire to visit the City of the Saints by the voluminous travel accounts provided by the forty-niners.

Furthermore, whereas prior to 1849 only Missourians and residents of Illinois had had close and neighborly contact with the Mormon lifestyle and customs, gold-rushers from every part of the nation were now able to observe and report to their families and to their hometown newspapers about the strange beliefs and practical behavior of the Utah pioneers. This general dissemination of knowledge about the Saints, their supposed unpatriotic and subversive statements and attitudes, and their open practice of many wives, contributed to the popular demand that the twin relics of slavery and the polygamous theocracy of the Mormon people be obliterated from the American landscape. The doctrine of polygamy especially was so abhorrent to the thinking of most Americans that it became the issue around which anti-Mormons and political opportunists could rally. Emigrant diaries and letters confirmed the practice as seen by unbelieving eyes and added fuel to the fires soon to be stoked by the leaders of the new Republican Party.

The inflammatory rhetoric of Mormon leaders in denouncing the Missouri and Illinois mobs and the obvious combination of church and state under the strong theocratic control of Brigham Young led critical emigrants to press demands that something be done to "Americanize" the Mormons. Gentile businessmen, newly aware of financial rewards in Salt Lake City, and federal officials, looking to Utah for political appointments, were pleased that national pressure resulted in the formation of Utah Territory rather than the establishment of a State of Deseret. Although the Washington administration bowed to the inevitable by appointing Brigham Young as governor, the judiciary was placed in the safe hands of Gentile officials. Slater, Goodell, and Langworthy, plus all the lesser emigrant publicists, were among the first to agitate for the kind of tight control of Mormondom which eventually led President James Buchanan to send an army to Utah. The Mormon reaction to outside pressure and the unrelenting attacks by former gold rush visitors may have had some influence in the later conception and massacre of a group of Missouri emigrants at Mountain Meadows by fearful and enraged Mormon settlers.

The gold rush emigrants who chose to travel to California by way of Salt Lake City were usually the least well-prepared, the latecomers who feared to tackle the snows of the Sierra Nevadas, the ones who became ill along the way, a few curious sightseers, or the argumentative who needed courts of law to settle their difficulties. It is interesting to speculate on what would have happened to the Mormon settlement if these adventurers had chosen to follow the Oregon and California trails via Fort Hall. Because of the strong commitment of the Saints to their new mountain home, it is doubtful that they would have moved en masse to California. Nevertheless, many more of those weak in the faith and attracted by the stories of golden fortunes would very likely have been sucked into the flow. The history of the Mormon church in California might have been different if hundreds of Saints had decided to cast their lot with the gold diggers. On the other hand, a number of wayfarers who visited in Salt Lake City converted to the new gospel and never reached the land of their early heart's desire.

With Salt Lake City established as a mercantile crossroads where supplies and relief could be obtained, the national government seized the opportunity to use the Mormon settlement as a base for further exploration of the far west. Captain Stansbury's survey of the Great Salt Lake was first, but soon other parties sought possible transcontinental routes for railroads and explored uncharted areas of the Great Basin. The City of the Saints was a convenient place of succor and rest for the army engineers; their official reports helped educate the eastern establishment about Mormon society and its practical accomplishments. Many of the published reports were quite favorable to the Saints, as were the two written by Stansbury and Gunnison.

The interaction between 25,000 gold rush emigrants and several thousand Mormon pioneers on the shores of America's great inland salt sea during 1849 and 1850 changed American history. The emigrants' written reports and diaries and letters, distributed far and wide, broke the isolation of the Mormon settlers and focused national attention once again on the "Mormon problem." Hidden away in the West, the Saints continued to build their City of Zion until political pressures against their unorthodox views and practices, which had been widely advertised by emigrant observers, led to action by the federal government. But to Saint and Gentile alike during the two summers of the gold rush years, their interaction involved economic and social exchange of benefit and interest to both in the shadow of the everlasting hills at the Mormon Halfway House.

NOTES

Chapter 1. Salt Lake Settlement

1. The narrative concerned with early Mormon history and the settlement of Salt Lake Valley is based in part on Arrington and Bitton, *The Mormon Experience*, pp. 83–105.

2. *New York Journal of Commerce*, Nov. 29, 1848, quoted in Bieber, "California Gold Mania," p. 19.

3. U.S. Congress, House, *Message from the President of the United States to the Two Houses of Congress*, p. 62.

4. W. Johnson, *The Forty-niners*, p. 38.

5. As quoted in Bieber, "California Gold Mania," p. 21.

6. *New York Tribune,* Jan. 23, 1849; Dec. 11, 1848.

7. Sexton, ed., *The Foster Family*, p. 42.

8. Hudson, Papers, J. H. Shearman to Benjamin Hudson, Jan. 26, 1849.

9. *New York Tribune*, Jan. 4, 1849.

10. Johnson, *The Forty-niners*, p. 46.

11. Stewart, *The California Trail*, p. 224.

12. Hudson, Papers, Constitution of the Colony Guard.

13. Kiefer, ed., "Over Barren Plains and Rock-Bound Mountains," p. 1.

14. Porter, *Aerial Navigation*, pp. 6–16.

15. John Smith, Papers.

16. Harmon, Diary, p. 48.

17. Brooks, ed., *On the Mormon Frontier* 2: 380.

18. "First General Epistle of the First Presidency of the Church of Jesus Christ of Latter-day Saints, from the Great Salt Lake Valley, to the Saints scattered throughout the Earth," from *New York Herald*, June 22, 1849, *The Latter-day Saints' Millennial Star* 11: 288 (hereafter cited as *Millennial Star*).

19. Judd, Autobiography, p. 19.

20. Brooks, ed., *A Mormon Chronicle* 1: 109.

21. Hale, Journal, p. 17.

22. Conover, Autobiography.

23. Robinson, Autobiography, p. 29.

24. Hancock, Autobiography, p. 43.

25. "First General Epistle," *Millennial Star* 11: 228.

26. Heward, History, p. 40.

27. Harmon, Diary, p. 24.

28. Brooks, *A Mormon Chronicle* 1: 88–90.

29. Ashby, ed., *Autobiography*, p. 23.

30. Sessions, Diary, p. 57.

31. Brooks, *On the Mormon Frontier* 1: 372.

32. McDiarmid, Letters.

33. J. S. Brown, *Life of a Pioneer*, p. 120.

34. History of Brigham Young, 1849, p. 69.

35. *Millennial Star* (1849) 11: 230, 247; Arrington, *Great Basin Kingdom*, pp. 58–62.

36. J. S. Brown, *Life of a Pioneer*, pp. 121–23.

Chapter 2.   Mormons Along the Overland

1. Jensen, "The Greenwood-Sublette Cutoff of the Oregon Trail," p. vi.

2. Stewart, *The California Trail*, pp. 245–46.

3. Evans, Journal, or, a Trip to California, p. 121.

4. Stewart, *The California Trail*, p. 246.

5. Morgan, "The Mormon Ferry on the North Platte," pp. 111–12.

6. Sawyer, *Way Sketches*, p. 39.

7. Harmon, Diary, June 20, 1847.

8. Morgan, "The Ferries of the Forty-Niners," Pt. 2, p. 145–52. A year later the Mormon crew left Salt Lake City two weeks earlier, but they still met an emigrant party that had already crossed the river on May 15.

9. Morgan, "Letters by Forty-Niners," p. 107.

10. Morgan, "The Mormon Ferry on the North Platte," p. 113.

11. Johnston, *Experiences of a Forty-niner*, June 3, 1849, entry.

12. D. Jagger, Diary, as quoted in Morgan, "The Ferries of the Forty-Niners," Pt. 1, p. 25.

13. Samuel F. McCoy, *Pioneering on the Plains*, as quoted in Morgan, "The Ferries of the Forty-Niners," Pt. 1, p. 29.

14. B. R. Biddle, *Illinois Journal*, Springfield, Ill., Dec. 11, 1849, as quoted in Morgan, "The Ferries of the Forty-Niners," Pt. 1, p. 23.

15. Read and Gaines, eds., *Gold Rush*, p. 1255, from Doctor [T. G.] Caldwell, "Notes of a Journey to California by Fort Hall Route, June to Oct^r, 1849–Found in Mountains" [copies by J. Goldsborough Bruff]; David Pease, Diary, as quoted in Morgan, "The Ferries of the Forty-Niners," Pt. 1, p. 21; W. Kelly, *Across the Rocky Mountains from New York to California*, pp. 174–76; David Cosad, Diary, as quoted in Morgan, "The Ferries of the Forty-Niners," Pt. 1, p. 17; B. R. Biddle, *Illinois Journal*, Springfield, Ill., Dec. 11, 1849, as quoted in Morgan, "The Ferries of the Forty-Niners," Pt. 1, p. 22; Jacob, Record, p. 73.

16. Benson, Diary.

17. T. Clark, ed., *Gold Rush Diary*, July 15, 1849.

18. Read and Gaines, *Gold Rush*, p. 44.

19. "Letter from George A. Smith to Orson Hyde, Camp of Israel, Spring Creek, 345 miles from Winter Quarters, August 21st, 1849," *Millennial Star* 11: 348–49.

20. Morgan, "The Ferries of the Forty-Niners," Pt. 1, pp. 12–31, gives a careful and detailed description of the Mormon Ferry on the Platte; supplemental materials may be found in Reid, *Law for the Elephant*, pp. 312–20, and Unruh, *The Plains Across*, p. 260.

21. George Johnson, Papers, as quoted in Morgan, "The Ferries of the Forty-Niners," Pt. 1, p. 20.

22. Prichet, Notes of a Trip to California, p. 41.

23. Read and Gaines, eds., *Gold Rush*, p. 1255.

24. Reid, *Law for the Elephant*, p. 313.

25. Brooks, ed., *A Mormon Chronicle* 1: 112.

26. Harmon, Diary, p. 27.

27. Johnston, *Experiences of a Forty-niner*, p. 152.

28. Morgan, "The Ferries of the Forty-Niners," Pt. 3, Sec. 1, pp. 52–53.

29. Hamelin, Overland Diaries, p. 40.

30. Foster, California Pioneers of 1849, p. 52; Trowbridge, ed., *Pioneer Days*, p. 110.

31. Morgan, "The Ferries of the Forty-Niners," Pt. 3, Sec. 2, pp. 200.

32. Carter, comp., *Life of Charles Sperry*, p. 446.

33. Darwin, Journals.

34. Stephens, *Life Sketches*, p. 12.

35. Hamelin, Overland Diaries, p. 40.

36. Eaton, *The Overland Trail*, pp. 189–90.

37. Morgan, "The Ferries of the Forty-Niners," Pt. 1, pp. 25.

38. Morgan, "The Ferries of the Forty-Niners," Pt. 3, Sec. 2, pp. 167–203; Stewart, *The California Trail*, p. 247; B. Clark, Diary, Mattes and Kirk, eds., "From Ohio to California in 1849," pp. 318, 403.

39. P. C. Tiffany, Diary, as quoted in Morgan, "The Ferries of the Forty-Niners," Pt. 3, Sec. 2, p. 174.

40. Amos Steck, Diary, as quoted in Morgan, "The Ferries of the Forty-Niners," Pt. 3, Sec. 2, pp. 192.

41. Mattes and Kirk, eds., "From Ohio to California," p. 403.

42. Steck, Diary, as quoted in Morgan, "The Ferries of the Forty-Niners," Pt. 3, Sec. 2, pp. 192.

43. Stewart, *The California Trail*, p. 230.

44. J. E. Brown, *Memoirs of a Forty-niner*, p. 20; Scamehorn, ed., *The Buckeye Rovers in the Gold Rush*, p. 46.

45. Scamehorn, ed., *The Buckeye Rovers in the Gold Rush*, p. 47.

46. Hixson, Diary, pp. 27–28.

47. Reid, *Law for the Elephant*, p. 97.

48. Giffen, ed., *The Diaries of Peter Decker*, p. 110.

49. Maynard, Diary of Overland Trip, Aug. 1, 1850.

50. Judge H. S. Brown, Statement of Early Days of Cal., pp. 1–2.

51. Stansbury, Journal, June 5, 8, 1849.

52. Stewart, *The California Trail*, pp. 229, 238.

53. J. W. Wood, Diary, July 21, 1849.

54. Stansbury, Journal, July 27, 1849.

55. Brooks, ed., *A Mormon Chronicle* 1: 111, 113.

56. *Millennial Star* Aug. 19, 1849, 11: 365.

57. Stephens, *Life Sketches*, p. 12.

58. Stansbury, Journal, Aug. 6, 1849.

59. *Millennial Star* 11: 377.

60. Ibid., p. 345.

61. Sargent, ed., *Seeking the Elephant*, p. 159.

62. Ibid., Preface.

63. Appleby, Autobiography and Journal, p. 261.

64. Gifford, Autobiography, p. 10.

65. Whipple, Journal, p. 90.

66. Fish, Autobiography, p. 4.

67. McCall, *The Great California Trail*, p. 48; Stephens, *Life Sketches*, p. 12.

68. Wilson, Original Letters, July 29, 1850; McCall, *The Great California Trail*, pp. 48, 50.

69. Morgan, "Letters by Forty-Niners," Letter from A. P. Josselyn, p. 105; Wells, Letters, July 20, 1849.

70. J. A. Johnson, Note Book, July 5, 1849.

71. Wilson, Original Letters, July 29, 1850.

72. Gunnison, *The Mormons*, p. 64.

73. Morgan, "Letters by Forty-Niners," Josselyn, p. 105; Hillyer, Journal, p. 46; Sexton, ed., *The Foster Family*, pp. 38–39.

74. *Millennial Star* 11: 344.

75. Brooks, ed., *A Mormon Chronicle* 1: 112.

76. Morgan, "Letters by Forty-Niners," Josselyn, p. 105; Sexton, ed., *The Foster Family*, pp. 38–39; Hillyer, Journal, p. 46.

77. Batchelder, Journal of a Tour, pp. 76–78; Joseph A. Stuart, *My Roving Life*, vol. 1, p. 52.

78. Read and Gaines, eds., *Gold Rush*, p. 132.

79. Goldsmith, *Overland in Forty-nine*, p. 54.

80. Langworthy, *Scenery of the Plains*, p. 113.

81. Stegner, *The Gathering of Zion*, p. 170.

82. Hillyer, Journal, p. 46.

83. *Deseret News*, July 20, 1850.

84. Slater, *Fruits of Mormonism*, pp. 4, 8, 11.

85. Journal History, Dec. 24, 1849, p. 2; History of Brigham Young, 1849, p. 97.

86. Bond, Diary, p. 17.

87. Korns, ed., *West From Fort Bridger*, p. 224.

88. Abbey, *California*, p. 38.

89. John Wood, Journal, p. 39.

90. Benson, Diary, p. 48.

91. T. Clark, ed., *Off at Sunrise*, pp. 59–60.

92. Morgan, "Letters by Forty-Niners," Letter of Beeson Townsend, p. 111.

93. Crane, Journal, July 8, 9, 1852.

94. Eaton, *The Overland Trail*, p. 203.

95. Sexton, ed., *The Foster Family*, p. 44; T. Clark, ed., *Off at Sunrise*, p. 62; Paden, ed., *Journal of Madison Berryman Moorman*, pp. 48, Preface.

96. Shields, Journal, p. 104.

97. Langworthy, *Scenery of the Plains*, p. 82.

98. Carr, *Pioneer Days in California*, p. 45.

99. Doyle, Journals and Letters of Simon Doyle, p. 38.

100. Hamelin, Overland Diaries, p. 47.

101. McBride, Journal of an Overland Trip, June 26, 1850.

102. History of Brigham Young, 1849, p. 149.

103. Korns, *West from Fort Bridger*, pp. 224–29.

104. Pulsipher, Diary, p. 27.

105. *Deseret News*, July 20, 1850.

106. Stansbury, Journal, p. 91.

107. Whipple, Journal, p. 91.

108. *Millennial Star* 12: 350.

Chapter 3.   City of the Saints

1. T. Clark, ed., *Off at Sunrise*, p. 63; Morgan, ed., "Letters by Forty-Niners," p. 109.

2. Hunter, *Brigham Young*, pp. 205, 212–14, 243–44.

3. History of Brigham Young, Oct. 1849, p. 156.

4. Debow, *Compendium, United States*, p. 332.

5. Arrington, *Great Basin Kingdom*, p. 68; *Frontier Guardian*, Sept. 5, 1849.

6. History of Brigham Young, 1850, p. 88.

7. Langworthy, *Scenery of the Plains*, p. 83.

8. J. L. Smith, Journal, pp. 17–18.

9. Journal History, letter from Brigham Young to Orson Hyde, July 20, 1849.

10. C. Ferguson, *California Gold Fields*, pp. 44–46.

11. Morgan, ed., "Letters by Forty-Niners," Josselyn, p. 102.

12. *Deseret News*, June 15–Aug. 17, 1850.

13. Unruh, *The Plains Across*, p. 308.

14. "From Lake Erie to the Pacific," p. 17.

15. *Millennial Star*, 11: 339.

16. Eaton, *The Overland Trail*, p. 205; *Western Reserve Chronicle*, Warren, Trumbull Co., Ohio, Oct. 10, 1849; Sargent, ed., *Seeking the Elephant*, p. 153; Hillyer, Journal, p. 47; Gould, Diary, Aug. 7, 1849.

17. History of Brigham Young, 1850, p. 60.

18. Langworthy, *Scenery of the Plains*, p. 90.

19. Beatie, The First in Nevada, p. 1.

20. Stansbury, *Exploration and Survey*, p. 129.

21. W. Kelly, *An Excursion to California*, p. 223.

22. McBride, Journal of an Overland Trip, June 26, 1850.

23. Morgan, "Letters by Forty-Niners," from *Frontier Guardian*, Feb. 30, 1850, p. 110, and Squires, p. 109; see also John Wood, *Journal*, p. 58.

24. Storm, ed., *"A Pretty Fair View of the Eliphent"*, p. 29; Carr, *Pioneer Days in California*, p. 45; Bloom, Journal, p. 26; Williams, ed., "Overland to California," p. 328.

25. Stansbury, *Exploration and Survey*, p. 128.

26. Morgan, ed., "Letters by Forty-Niners," Josselyn, p. 104.

27. From Lake Erie to the Pacific, p. 19.

28. Newcomb, Journal of a Trip to California, p. 113.

29. Doyle, Journals and Letters of Simon Doyle, p. 39; see also Benson, Diary, p. 52.

30. Morgan, ed., "Letters by Forty-Niners," from *Frontier Guardian*, Feb. 20, 1850, p. 110.

31. Whipple, Journal, pp. 94–95.

32. Smucker, ed., *History of the Mormons*, p. 310; see also Hudson, Papers, letter of Oct. 1849.

33. Heaston, ed., *From Mississippi to California*, p. 76; Pettit, *Biography of Edwin Pettit*, p. 10.

34. W. Kelly, *An Excursion to California*, pp. 228–29.

35. Benson, Diary, p. 52.

36. Sargent, ed., *Seeking the Elephant*, p. 153.

37. Newcomb, Journal of a Trip to California, pp. 115–16; Smucker, *History of the Mormons*, p. 314.

38. Muench, ed., *The Kilgore Journal*, p. 36.

39. Williams, ed., Overland to California, p. 328.

40. T. Clark, ed., *Off at Sunrise*, p. 67.

41. Morgan, ed., "Letters by Forty-Niners," Squires, p. 109.

42. Evershed, "The Gold Rush Journal of Thomas Evershed," p. 24.

43. History of Brigham Young, 1849, p. 95; Early History, p. 85.

44. History of Brigham Young, 1849, p. 142.

45. Sortore, *Biography and Early Life Sketch*, p. 5.

46. Stephens, *Life Sketches*, pp. 14–15.

47. Langworthy, *Scenery of the Plains*, p. 90.

48. History of Brigham Young, 1849, p. 142.

49. W. Kelly, *An Excursion to California*, p. 228.

50. Doyle, Journals and Letters of Simon Doyle, p. 41.

51. W. Kelly, *An Excursion to California*, p. 227.

52. T. Clark, ed., *Gold Rush Diary*, p. 17.

53. Morgan, ed., "Letters by Forty-Niners," Squires, p. 109; Shields, Journal, p. 104.

54. Smucker, ed., *History of the Mormons*, p. 314.

55. Heaston, ed., *From Mississippi to California*, pp. 75–76; Black, Sketch, p. 4; From Lake Erie to the Pacific, p. 19; Newcomb, Journal of a Trip to California, p. 114; Benson, Diary, p. 52.

56. Stansbury, *Exploration and Survey*, p. 128.

57. Journal History, Sept. 24, 30, 1848; *Millennial Star* 11: 228.

58. Langworthy, *Scenery of the Plains*, p. 89.

59. *Millennial Star* 11: 228.

60. Morgan, ed., "Letters by Forty-Niners," John B. Hazlip, p. 100.

61. Bloom, Journal, p. 25.

62. Greenwood, Journal, p. 23.

63. Doyle, *Journals and Letters of Simon Doyle*, p. 39; Hovey, Journal, p. 199; *Millennial Star* 12: 120.

64. W. Kelly, *An Excursion to California*, p. 227; Shields, Journal, p. 104.

65. Muench, ed., *The Kilgore Journal*, p. 37; Benson, Diary, p. 52.

66. Stansbury, *Exploration and Survey*, p. 141; Haight, Journal, p. 47.

67. Heaston, ed., *From Mississippi to California*, p. 76; Morgan, ed., "Letters by Forty-Niners," Squire, p. 109; Summers, Miners' and Travellers' Pocket Letter Book, p. 6; Williams, ed., Overland to California, p. 327; Smucker, *History of the Mormons*, p. 310.

68. McDiarmid, Letters, July 28, 1850.

69. Morgan, ed., "Letters by Forty-Niners," Gold Mines, p. 116.

70. Lorton, Diary, p. 176.

71. T. Clark, ed., *Gold Rush Diary*, p. 177.

72. Summers, Miners' and Travellers' Pocket Letter Book, p. 6.

73. C. Kelly, *Salt Deseret Trails*, p. 127.

74. Stansbury, *Exploration and Survey*, p. 141.

75. History of Brigham Young, 1850, p. 89.

76. Knowlton, "The Early History of Agriculture in Utah," pp. 89, 92.

77. DeBow, *Compendium*, pp. 171–74.

78. Ibid., pp. 170–71.

79. Muench, ed., *The Kilgore Journal*, p. 37.

80. T. Clark, ed., *Gold Rush Diary*, p. 177.

81. McKeeby, Memoirs, p. 27.

82. Stephens, *Life Sketches*, p. 13.

83. Judd, Autobiography, p. 19.

84. Morris, Autobiography, p. 60.

85. Spencer, Biography of Daniel Spencer, pp. 9–10.

86. History of Brigham Young, 1848, p. 30.

87. *Millennial Star* 12: 366; Brooks, ed., *A Mormon Chronicle* 1: 106, 110.

88. W. Kelly, *An Excursion to California*, p. 229.

89. T. Clark, ed., *Gold Rush Diary*, p. 178.

90. Mattes, *The Great Platte River Road*, pp. 46–47; W. Call, Recollections, p. 10.

91. From Lake Erie to the Pacific, p. 18.

92. C. Ferguson, *California Gold Fields*, p. 45.

93. McDiarmid, Letters, July 28, 1850.

94. Sortore, *Biography and Early Life Sketch*, p. 5.

95. John Wood, *Journal of John Wood*, p. 59.

96. Ellenbecker, *Jayhawkers of Death Valley*, p. 15; Gould, Diary, Aug. 7, 1849.

97. Stephens, *Life Sketches*, p. 13; T. Clark, ed., *Off at Sunrise*, pp. 62–63.

98. Sargent, ed., *Seeking the Elephant*, p. 154.

99. Johnston, *Overland to California*, p. 120.

100. Black, *Sketch*, p. 4.

101. Lewis, Overland Diary, p. 19.

102. Johnston, *Overland to California*, p. 127.

103. Whitman, Journal, Bk. 1, p. 112.

104. Allen, Diary, p. 6.

105. Langworthy, *Scenery of the Plains*, p. 91.

106. Doyle, Journals and Letters of Simon Doyle, p. 39.

107. Sargent, ed., *Seeking the Elephant*, p. 156.

108. Senter, Letters, p. 11.

109. T. Clark, ed., *Off at Sunrise*, p. 62.

110. Paden, ed., *Journal of Madison Berryman Moorman*, July 20, 1859; Holtzhueter, ed., "From Waupun to Sacramento in 1849," p. 238; C. Taylor, Diary, July 29, 1850; Mighels, *How Many Miles to St. Jo?*, Hamelin, Overland Diaries, p. 43.

111. J. Richards, Reminiscences, p. 36; Brooks, ed., *On the Mormon Frontier* 2: 372.

112. Sessions, Diary, pp. 57–58.

113. From Lake Erie to the Pacific, pp. 21–22; Bloom, Journal, p. 26.

114. Shield, Journal of a Trip, p. 107; *Millennial Star* 12: 351.

115. As quoted in Mattes, *Great Platte River Road*, p. 36.

116. Gould, Diary, Aug. 14, 1849.

117. Johnston, *Overland to California*, p. 122; C. Kelly, "Gold Seekers on the Hastings Cutoff," p. 47; Morgan, "Letters by Forty-Niners," M.C.H., p. 102; Judd, Autobiography, p. 19; Journal History, July 20, 1849; *Frontier Guardian*, Sept. 19, 1849; Allen, Diary, p. 5; J. L. Smith, Diary, p. 3; Hillyer, Journal, p. 47; Orvis, Journal, p. 19; *Western Reserve Chronicle*, Oct. 10, 1849.

118. Hall, Diary of a Forty-niner, p. 14; Gabriel, ed., *A Frontier Lady*, p. 29; Judge H. S. Brown, Statement of Early days of Cal., p. 1; Abbey, *California*, p. 40; T. Clark, ed., *Gold Rush Diary*, p. 180.

119. W. Taylor, "Pioneer Reminiscences."

120. Heaston, ed., *From Mississippi to California*, p. 77.

121. Sargent, ed., *Seeking the Elephant*, p. 155; C. Taylor, Diary, Aug. 14, 1849.

122. Lorton, Diary, p. 176.

123. Brooks, ed., *On the Mormon Frontier* 2: 372–78.

124. Morgan, "Letters by Forty-Niners," Gold Mines, p. 114.

125. *Millennial Star* 11: 229; *Frontier Guardian*, May 1, 1850; Stephens, *Life Sketches*, p. 16.

126. Journal History, Mar. 6, May 15, 1848; Arrington, *Great Basin Kingdom*, p. 72.

127. W. Kelly, *An Excursion to California*, p. 222; Lewis, Overland Diary, p. 19.

128. Lund, comps., *Pulsipher Family History Book*, p. 22.

129. Morgan, "Letters by Forty-Niners," Josselyn, p. 103.

130. L. Brown, Journal, Vol. 1, May 28, 1850; Millington, Diary, June 4, 1850; Newcomb, Journal of a Trip to California, p. 118; Original Manuscript Letters, letter of Apr. 15, 1850; Shields, Journal, p. 104; Clay, Letter; Pearson, Recollections of a California '49'er; Nelson Slater, *Fruits of Mormonism*, p. 11; Unruh, *The Plains Across*, p. 323.

131. History of Brigham Young, June 24, 1849, p. 93; *Millennial Star* 11: 339–40; *Deseret News*, June 29, 1850; *Millennial Star* 12: July 1850, p. 350.

132. Hovey, Journal, p. 195.

133. *Millennial Star* 11: 231.

134. J. S. Brown, *Life of a Pioneer*, p. 124.

135. Ibid.; Pulsipher, Diary, p. 26; F. Hammond, "In Early Days," p. 521; *Frontier Guardian*, Sept. 5, 1849; Smucker, *History of the Mormons*, p. 313.

136. Journal History, Sept. 6, 1850.

137. Robinson, Autobiography, p. 72.

138. *Deseret News*, Sept. 7, 1850.

139. Foster, California Pioneers of 1849, p. 56.

140. *Millennial Star* 11: 233.

141. Clay, Letter.

142. Stephens, *Life Sketches*, p. 15.

143. Millington, Diary, June 4, 1850.

144. Read and Gaines, eds., *Gold Rush*, p. 65.

145. History of Brigham Young, July 6, 1849, p. 99.

146. *Millennial Star* 11: 231.

147. Journal History, Apr. 5, 1849, pp. 3–4.

148. *Millennial Star* 12: 244–45.

149. Arrington, *Great Basin Kingdom*, pp. 74–75; J. Kenneth Davies, "The Mormon Apostolic Argonauts."

150. B. Johnson, Autobiography, p. 124; Haight, Journal, p. 48.

Chapter 4. Great Basin Open Air Market

1. C. Crosby, Journal.

2. T. Clark, ed., *Gold Rush Diary*, p. 177.

3. Sargent, ed., *Seeking the Elephant*, p. 156; J. H. Widber, Statement, p. 3; Kane, *The Mormons*, p. 77; John Smith, Papers, Apr. 28, 1849.

4. B. Johnson, Autobiography, p. 123; Judd, Autobiography, p. 19; Gabriel, ed., *A Frontier Lady*, p. 29; Leany, Autobiography, p. 11; C. Stuart, Trip to California.

5. *Western Reserve Chronicle*, letter from John B. Chamberlain, Oct. 10, 1849.

6. Morgan, "Letters by Forty-Niners," M.C.H., p. 101; see also Silas Richards, Journal, p. 11; Hovey, Journal, p. 196; Sortore, *Biography and Early Life Sketch*, p. 4; W. Taylor, "Pioneer Reminiscences," p. 2; Ness, Journal, p. 12; Dundass, *Journal*, p. 40.

7. Heaston, ed., *From Mississippi to California*, p. 78.

8. James M. Hutchings, Diary, Sept. 7, 1849.

9. Paden, ed., *Journal of Madison Berryman Moorman*, July 20, 1850.

10. Wilson, "Original Letters from the Plains and Diggings," July 29, 1850; see also Cook, Reminiscences and Journal, n.p.; J. Richards, Reminiscences, p. 34; Wylly, Westward Ho, p. 44; Shinn, Journal Overland, Aug. 9–10, 1850.

11. Reid, *Law for the Elephant*, pp. 232–35; C. Taylor, Diary, July 29, 1850.

12. Carr, *Pioneer Days in California*, pp. 48–51.

13. Enos, Personal Recollections, eighth letter.

14. History of Brigham Young, July 1850, p. 59.

15. Slater, *Fruits of Mormonism*, p. 9.

16. Bloom, Journal, p. 26; C. Smith, Reminiscences, p. 24; Kiefer, ed., "Over Barren Plains and Rock-Bound Mountains," p. 24; Pulsipher, Diary, p. 28; Borrowman, Diary, May 1850.

17. *Deseret News*, June 29, 1850.

18. Langworthy, *Scenery of the Plains*, p. 102.

19. Hovey, Journal, pp. 205–6.

20. Sessions, Diary, p. 67.

21. Harker, Journal; see also Clay, Letter, Sept. 22, 1849; Brooks, ed., *On the Mormon Frontier* 2: 114, 354; *Millennial Star* 12: 119; Bancroft, *History of California*, p. 152; Hancock, Autobiography, p. 44; Ashby, *Autobiography*, p. 23; Hale, Journal, p. 13; B. Johnson, Autobiography, p. 123; Judd, Autobiography, p. 20; Albert Smith, Reminiscences; Smoot, Experience of a Mormon Wife, pp. 5–6; Kimball, *Heber C. Kimball*, p. 190.

22. Morris, Autobiography, p. 61.

23. *Journal of Discourses* 10: 247.

24. Benjamin Brown, "Testimonies for the Truth" (Liverpool, 1853), pp. 27–29, as quoted in Arrington, *Great Basin Kingdom*, pp. 67, 441.

25. McArthur, Autobiography, p. 61.

26. Holbrook, History, p. 96.

27. Allen, Diary, p. 5.

28. Hovey, Journal, pp. 193–94.

29. Jonathan Crosby, Autobiography, p. 29; Judge H. S. Brown, Statement of Early days of Cal., p. 1; Holdaway, *Biographical Sketch*, p. 3; *Frontier Guardian*, Sept. 5, 1849; Hales, Journal, p. 13; Edwards, Journal; Carter, comp., *Life of Charles Sperry*, p. 446.

30. Arrington, *Great Basin Kingdom*, p. 67.

31. *Frontier Guardian*, Sept. 5, 1849.

32. Lambert, Autobiography, p. 30.

33. B. Johnson, Autobiography, pp. 122–23.

34. Jonathan Crosby, Autobiography, p. 29.

35. Ward, ed., *A Fragment*, p. 61; Meeks, Journal, p. 71; Udell, *Incidents of Travel*, p. 25; L. Brown, Journal, July 28, 1849; Gardner, ed., *Alma Helaman Hale*, p. 11; *Millennial Star* 11: 342.

36. Hovey, Journal, p. 193; Lambert, Autobiography, p. 30; Robinson, Journal, p. 30; T. Clark, ed., *Off at Sunrise*, p. 65; Morgan, ed., "Letters by Forty-Niners," Townsend, p. 112.

37. Allen, Diary, p. 5.

38. Morris, Autobiography, pp. 62–63.

39. Chapman Duncan, Biography, p. 11A.

40. Judd, Autobiography, p. 20.

41. Storm, ed., "*A Pretty Fair View of the Eliphent*," p. 32; Dundass, Journal, p. 42; Hall, Diary of a Forty-niner, p. 12.

42. Wilson, "Original Letters from the Plains and Diggings," July 29, 1850; Allen, Diary, p. 6.

43. *Millennial Star* 12: 124.

44. Robinson, Journal, p. 125.

45. B. Johnson, Autobiography, p. 125.

46. History of Brigham Young, 1849, p. 143; J. L. Smith, Diary, p. 3; Ward, ed., *A Fragment*, p. 61.

47. L. Brown, Journal, July 28, 1849; Borrowman, Diary, June 1849, May 1850.

48. Sessions, Diary, p. 58.

49. W. Kelly, *An Excursion to California*, p. 222.

50. Stephens, *Life Sketches*, p. 13; Allen, Diary, p. 5; C. Smith, Reminiscences, p. 23.

51. Morgan, "Letters by Forty-Niners," Beeson Townsend, p. 112.

52. Leany, Autobiography, p. 11.

53. Langworthy, *Scenery of the Plains*, p. 91; J. L. Smith, Diary, p. 3.

54. Hancock, Autobiography, p. 44.

55. Udell, *Incidents of Travel*, p. 25.

56. Lewis, Overland Diary, p. 19; Paden, ed., *Journal of Madison Berryman Moorman*, July 22, 1850; Meeks, Journal, p. 70.

57. Johnston, *Overland to California*, p. 120.

58. Brooks, ed., *On the Mormon Frontier* 2: 355; Original Manuscript Letters, Letter of Apr. 15, 1850; McArthur, Autobiography, p. 62; Kelly, *An Excursion to California*, p. 222.

59. Cole, *Memoirs of Cornelius Cole*.

60. Millington, Diary, June 4, 1850.

61. Morgan, "Letters by Forty-Niners," Hazlip, p. 100.

62. Hancock, Autobiography, p. 44.

63. Johnston, *Overland to California*, p. 120.

64. Sargent, ed., *Seeking the Elephant*, p. 156.

65. Thissell, *Crossing the Plains in '49*, p. 104; Ellenbecker, *Jayhawkers of Death Valley*, p. 15.

66. Stephens, *Life Sketches of a Jayhawker*, p. 13.

67. Ashby, *Autobiography*, p. 23.

68. Hale, Journal, p. 12.

69. Millington, Diary, June 4, 1850.

70. Morgan, ed., "Letters by Forty-Niners," Townsend, p. 112.

71. Thissell, *Crossing the Plains in '49*, pp. 34–35.

72. W. Kelly, *An Excursion to California*, p. 223.

73. C. Smith, Reminiscences, p. 24; Morgan, ed., "Letters by Forty-Niners," Townsend, p. 112.

74. Kleiser, Autobiography, p. 35.

75. Meeks, Journal, p. 70.

76. B. Johnson, Autobiography, p. 125.

77. C. Ferguson, *California Gold Fields*, p. 46; T. Clark, ed., *Off at Sunrise*, p. 65.

78. *Frontier Guardian*, Sept. 15, 1849; Hall, Diary of a Forty Niner, p. 14.

79. Lorton, Diary, p. 176.

80. *Millennial Star* 11: 341.

81. Ibid. 12: 350.

82. Brooks, ed., *A Mormon Chronicle* 1: 110.

83. Morgan, ed., "Letters by Forty-Niners," Townsend, p. 112; Wyman, ed., *California Emigrant Letters,* p. 62; *Early History,* Sept. 1850, p. 113; McKeeby, Memoirs, p. 29; Millington, Diary, June 4, 1850; Kiefer, ed., "Over Barren Plains and Rock-Bound Mountains," p. 24; Whitman, Journal, Bk. 2, p. 31; Lambert, Autobiography, p. 30.

84. Morgan, ed., "Letters by Forty-Niners," Townsend, p. 112; Journal History, July 20, 1849; Eaton, *The Overland Trail,* p. 206; L. Brown, Journal, July 28, 1849; Hall, Diary of a Forty Niner, p. 14; Brooks, ed., *A Mormon Chronicle* 1: 110; Wyman, ed., *California Emigrant Letters,* p. 62; p. 62; Hermann, ed., "Three Gold Rush Letters," pp. 63–64.

85. *Frontier Guardian,* Nov. 13, 1850.

86. A. J. McCall, *The Great California Trail,* p. 60.

87. Mattes, *Great Platte River Road,* p. 38; Appleby, Autobiography and Journal, p. 261.

88. T. Clark, ed., *Gold Rush Diary,* p. 177.

89. W. Kelly, *An Excursion to California,* p. 227.

90. Darwin, Journals, p. 198; Whitman, Journal, Bk. 1, p. 112; Evershed, "The Gold Rush Journal of Thomas Evershed," p. 26; Morgan, ed., "Letters by Forty-Niners," Hazlip, p. 100.

91. Wooster, *The Gold Rush,* p. 12; King, Journal, n.p.

92. Because the price of flour and wheat was of major concern to all emigrants, the overland diaries are filled with such information. The following citations only represent examples of the changes in price that occurred: *Frontier Guardian,* Mar. 7, May 30, 1849, Nov. 13, 1850; *Millennial Star* 11: 228, 338, 365; Original Manuscript Letters, Oct. 14, 1849; Evershed, "The Gold Rush Journal of Thomas Evershed," p. 26; Adams, Biography, p. 14; Brooks, ed., *A Mormon Chronicle* 1: 114; Morgan, ed., "Letters by Forty-Niners," Hazlip, p. 100; Hall, Diary of a Forty Niner, p. 14; Hammond, "In Early Days," p. 520; Lorton, Diary, p. 176; Booth, En Route to California, p. 14; L. Brown, Journal, July 13, 1850; Stansbury, Journal, June 30, 1850; Whitman, Journal, Bk. 1, p. 112; Hudson, Papers, letter Apr. 2. 1850; Ashley, Diary, p. 11; Delano, *Journal,* p. 1; Newcomb, Journal of a Trip to California, p. 117; *Millennial Star* 12: 300, 350; McKeeby, Memoirs, p. 28; History of Brigham Young, 1849, pp. 99, 1850, pp. 58–59.

93. History of Brigham Young, 1849, p. 99.

94. Flint, Diary, p. 51; Crane, Journal, p. 56.

95. Wyman, ed., *California Emigrant Letters,* p. 62; Hall, Diary of a Forty Niner, p. 14; Morgan, ed., "Letters by Forty-Niners," Hazlip, p. 100; Heaston, ed., *From Mississippi to California,* p. 76; Brooks, ed., *A Mormon Chronicle* 1: 111; T. Clark, ed., *Gold Rush Diary,* p. 177; Evershed, "Gold Rush Journal," p. 26; Orvis, Journal, p. 19; Hermann, ed., "Three Gold Rush Letters," p. 64; Morgan, ed., "Letters by Forty-Niners," Josselyn, p. 103, and Gold Mines, p. 115; *Millennial Star* 12: 300, 350; Newcomb, Journal of a Trip to California, p. 117; McDiarmid, Letters, July 28, 1850; Delano, Journal, p. 1; Millington, Diary, June 4, 1850; Whitman, Journal, Bk. 1, p. 112, Bk. 2, p. 33; Booth, En Route to California, p. 14; Abbey, *California,* p. 39; Muench, ed., *The Kilgore Journal,* p. 39; McBride, Journal of An Overland Trip, June 26, 1850; Kiefer, ed., Over Barren Plains and Rock-Bound Mountains, p. 24; Wooster, *The Gold Rush,* p. 9; McKeeby, Memoirs, p. 28;

Frontier Guardian, Nov. 13, 1850; Original Manuscript Letters, Apr. 15, 16, 1850; History of Brigham Young, 1849, p. 99, 1850, p. 29; Bloom, Journal, p. 26.

96. Smucker, ed., *History of the Mormons*, p. 311; see also Black, Sketch, p. 4; W. Kelly, *An Excursion to California*, p. 226.

97. *Millennial Star* 11: 367; see also Hovey, Journal, p. 198.

98. *Millennial Star* 12: 86; Hogan, History, p. 16.

99. Lorton, Diary, p. 176.

100. Journal History, Nov. 21, 1849.

101. History of Brigham Young, 1850, p. 82.

102. Harris, *An Unwritten Chapter*, p. 32.

103. *Millennial Star* 12. 86.

104. Harris, *An Unwritten Chapter*, p. 33.

105. Morgan, ed., "Letters by Forty-Niners," Gold Mines, p. 115.

106. Newcomb, Journal of a Trip to California, p. 117; *Millennial Star* 12: 350–51; Reese, Mormon Station; Verdenal, Journal, p. 30.

107. Frederick, *Ben Holladay*, pp. 28–33; *Deseret News*, Dec. 15, 1851.

108. Brooks, ed., *On the Mormon Frontier*, 2: 381.

109. Slater, *Fruits of Mormonism*, pp. 10–11.

110. *Deseret News*, June 22, 29, July 1, 6, 1850.

111. Crane, Journal, p. 59.

112. *Deseret News*, June 15, July 1, 6, Sept. 7, 1850.

113. F. Richards, Journal, p. 85.

114. Stansbury, *Exploration and Survey*, p. 143.

115. Morgan, ed., "Letters by Forty-Niners," Josselyn, p. 104.

Chapter 5.   Saints or Sinners?

1. Scamehorn, ed., *The Buckeye Rovers in the Gold Rush*, p. 47.

2. Shields, Journal, p. 108.

3. O. Jennings, Journal, p. 110.

4. McCall, *The Great California Trail in 1849*, p. 60.

5. Paden, ed., *Journal of Madison Berryman Moorman*, July 25, 1850.

6. Meeks, Journal, pp. 71–72.

7. Hogan, History, p. 17.

8. B. Johnson, Autobiography, pp. 125–26.

9. Caughey, ed., "Southwest from Salt Lake City in 1849," p. 170.

10. Judge H. S. Brown, Statement of Early days of Cal., p. 1; see also Shaw, *Eldorado*, p. 80.

11. J. Richards, Reminiscences, p. 34.

12. Stansbury, *Exploration and Survey*, p. 134; *Deseret News*, July 6, 1850.

13. Morgan, ed., "Letters by Forty-Niners," p. 99.

14. Langworthy, *Scenery of the Plains*, p. 98.

15. History of Brigham Young, 1849, pp. 102–3.

16. Greenwood, Journal, p. 23.

17. L. Brown, Journal, Mar. 9, 1851.

18. Unruh, *The Plains Across*, pp. 332–33; see also *Deseret News*, Aug. 7, 1852.

19. *Millennial Star* 11: 339.

20. Young, Diary, July 25, 1849.

21. Brooks, ed., *On the Mormon Frontier* 2: 525.

22. Morgan, ed., "Letters by Forty-Niners," *Missouri Courier*, p. 113.

23. McBride, Journal of an Overland Trip, June 28, 1850.

24. Bush, Letter.

25. C. Ferguson, *California Gold Fields*, p. 47.

26. Paden, ed., *Journal of Madison Berryman Moorman*, July 23, 1850.

27. Bloom, Journal, p. 27.

28. Carr, *Pioneer Days in California*, p. 45; Morgan, ed., "Letters by Forty-Niners," *Missouri Courier*, p. 114; Sortore, Biography and Early Life Sketch, p. 4; Booth, En Route to California, p. 14.

29. McCall, *The Great California Trail*, p. 48.

30. Johnston, *Overland to California*, p. 119.

31. Evershed, "The Gold Rush Journal of Thomas Evershed," p. 26.

32. T. Clark, ed., *Gold Rush Diary*, p. 178.

33. Evershed, "The Gold Rush Journal of Thomas Evershed," p. 26.

34. Heaston, ed., *From Mississippi to California*, p. 76; see also Newcomb, Journal of a Trip to California, p. 115.

35. Williams, ed., Overland to California, p. 329.

36. Gunnison, *The Mormons*, p. 66.

37. An earlier historian, Archer Hulbert, concluded, after examining a number of gold rush diaries, that the belief that emigrants were generally hostile to the Mormons was untrue as was the fact of specific allegations of wrongdoing. Hulbert, *Forty-Niners*, pp. viii–ix; History of Brigham Young, 1850, p. 25; *Liverpool Mercury*, Oct. 5, 1849; Wilson, Original Letters, July 29, 1850; John Wood, *Journal*, p. 59; Darwin, Journals, p. 197.

38. Flint, *Diary*, p. 48.

39. Haight, Diary, p. 61.

40. Lorton, Diary, p. 191.

41. *Millennial Star* 12: 28; see also Early History, p. 109, which quotes very favorable comments from a letter by Captain Howard Stansbury.

42. Mattes, *Great Platte River Road*, pp. 84–85, gives these estimates based on several journal entries.

43. Bancroft, *History of California*, p. 151.

44. Sortore, *Biography and Early Life Sketch*, p. 2.

45. Winchell, Crossing the Plains, p. 106; Morgan, ed., "Letters by Forty-Niners," C.H.M., p. 101.

46. Mattes, *Great Platte River Road*, p. 85; Journal History, July 14, 1849.

47. History of Brigham Young, 1849, p. 149, 1850, p. 92.

48. Pulsipher, Diary, p. 27.

49. *Western Reserve Chronicle*, Feb. 27, 1850.

50. Morrell, "Medicine of the Pioneer Period," p. 128.

51. Nash, Life Story, p. 6.

52. Leany, Autobiography, p. 11.

53. Appleby, Autobiography and Journal, p. 283.

54. Morgan, ed., "Letters by Forty-Niners," Townsend, p. 113; see also Gunnison, *The Mormons*, p. 65; Tompkins, Diary, p. 85; C. Crosby, Journal; Ferris, *Utah and the Mormons*, p. 196; *Western Reserve Chronicle*, Oct. 10, 1849; Read and Gains, eds., *Gold Rush*, p. 141.

55. History of Brigham Young, 1849, p. 88.

56. Hudson, Papers, letter Oct. 6, 1849; *Millennial Star* 12: 94.

57. Appleby, Autobiography and Journal, p. 283; Sessions, Diary, p. 59; Samuel Richards, Journal, p. 43; see also C. Ferguson, *California Gold Fields*, p. 48; Hillyer, Journal, p. 46; Bond, Diary, p. 18; Heaston, ed., *From Mississippi to California*, p. 74; Hovey, Journal, p. 195.

58. Wilson, Original Letters, July 29, 1850.

59. Jesse Crosby, Journal, p. 39.

60. Alter, ed., "The State of Deseret," pp. 75–76.

61. Ibid., pp. 84–113; Neff, *History of Utah*, p. 168.

62. W. Kelly, *An Excursion to California*, p. 230; Hoover, Diary, Aug. 19, 1849.

63. John Wood, *Journal*, p. 59; Morgan, ed., "Letters by Forty-Niners," *Frontier Guardian*, Feb. 20, 1850, p. 111.

64. Stansbury, *Exploration and Survey*, p. 123.

65. F. Richards, Journal, p. 22.

66. L. Brown, Journal, Jan. 8, 1851.

67. Pulsipher, Diary, p. 28.

68. Brooks, ed., *A Mormon Chronicle* 1: 107.

69. Bancroft, *History of Utah*, pp. 447–48.

70. *Deseret News*, July 1, 1850.

71. Ibid., July 20, 1850.

72. McDiarmid, Letters, July 28, 1850.

73. Flint, *Diary*, pp. 52–53.

74. Stansbury, *Exploration and Survey*, p. 134; Bancroft, *History of Utah*, p. 447.

75. T. Clark, ed., *Gold Rush Diary*, p. 178.

76. Hoover, Diary, Aug. 22, 1849; Hudson, Papers, letter Apr. 2, 1850.

77. Borrowman, Diary, June 24, 1849.

78. Ferris, *Utah and the Mormons*, p. 196.

79. Brooks, ed., *On the Mormon Frontier*, 2: 376.

80. Lorton, Diary, pp. 185–86.

81. Sessions, Diary, p. 58; Hamelin, Overland Diaries, p. 53.

82. W. Taylor, "Pioneer Reminiscences," p. 3.

83. Brooks, ed., *On the Mormon Frontier* 2: 370; see also T. Clark, ed., *Gold Rush Diary*, p. 178.

84. Lorenzo Brown, Journal, Jan. 12, 1851.

85. Bancroft, *History of Utah*, p. 448.

86. T. Clark, ed., *Gold Rush Diary*, p. 177; Alter, "The State of Deseret," pp. 171–74.

87. Brooks, ed., *On the Mormon Frontier* 2: 371–73, 375–76, 440.

88. *Governor's Message.*

89. Brooks, ed. *On the Mormon Frontier* 2: 371, 374.

90. Hudson, Papers, letter, July 20, 1850.

91. Brooks, ed., *On the Mormon Frontier,* 2: 375.

92. *Deseret News*, July 6, 1850.

93. Hudson, Papers, letter July 20, 1850.

94. *Deseret News*, July 6, 1850; Brooks, ed., *On the Mormon Frontier* 2: 377.

95. Brooks, ed., *On the Mormon Frontier* 2: 372.

96. Ibid., p. 378.

97. Brooks, ed., *On the Mormon Frontier* 2: 373–78.

98. Hoover, Diary, Aug. 16, 1849.

99. Brooks, ed., *On the Mormon Frontier* 2: 376.

100. Ibid., p. 374.

101. John Wood, *Journal,* p. 60.

102. Stansbury, *Exploration and Survey*, p. 131.

103. Brooks, ed., *On the Mormon Frontier* 2: 375.

104. Ibid., p. 371.

105. Ibid., p. 376; *Deseret News*, July 6, 1850.

106. Brooks, ed., *On the Mormon Frontier* 2: 373.

107. Ibid., p. 377.

Chapter 6. Taking in the Sights

1. Benson, Diary, p. 54; Mighels, *How Many Miles from St. Jo.?*, p. 19; Hudson, Papers, letter Apr. 2, 1850; Morgan, "Letters by Forty-Niners," Squire, p. 109.

2. Whitney, *History of Utah*, p. 336.

3. T. Clark, ed., *Off at Sunrise*, p. 65; Sargent, ed., *Seeking the Elephant*, p. 254; W. Kelly, *An Excursion to California*, p. 227; J. L. Smith, Diary, p. 3.

4. DeWolf, "Diary of the Overland Trail," p. 205.

5. Johnston, *Overland to California*, p. 123.

6. Holzhueter, ed., "From Waupun to Sacramento in 1849," p. 238; T. Clark, ed., *Off at Sunrise*, p. 65.

7. Johnston, Overland to California, p. 123.

8. Sargent, ed., *Seeking the Elephant*, p. 155.

9. W. Kelly, *An Excursion to California*, p. 228.

10. Benson, Diary, p. 54.

11. T. Clark, ed., *Off at Sunrise*, p. 65; see also Johnston, *Overland to California*, p. 122.

12. Hudson, Letters, Apr. 2, 1850; History of Brigham Young, 1850, pp. 32, 90.

13. Hendricks, Account of Conversion; see also Babcock, Reminiscences, p. 8; Brooks, ed., *On theMormon Frontier* 2: 376.

14. *Frontier Guardian*, Jan. 8, 1851.

15. *Deseret News*, Jan. 11, 1851.

16. Ibid., Mar. 22, 1851.

17. Clawson, Rambling Reminiscences, p. 95; see also Holzhueter, ed., "From Waupun to Sacramento in 1849," p. 238; C. Ferguson, *California Gold Fields*, p. 46.

18. Stephens, *Life Sketches of a Jayhawker of '49*, p. 16.

19. Hamelin, "The Overland Diaries," p. 43; Kilgore, Journal, p. 184; Langworthy, *Scenery of the Plains*, p. 113; Holzhueter, ed., "From Waupun to Sacramento in 1849," p. 238; Paden, ed., *Journal of Madison Berryman Moorman*, July 25, 1850.

20. Sargent, ed., *Seeking the Elephant*, p. 155.

21. Lewis, Overland Diary, p. 19.

22. John Wood, *Journal*, p. 61; Paden, ed., *Journal of Madison Berryman Moorman*, July 26, 1850; Gunnison, *The Mormons*, p. 51.

23. Morgan, ed., "Letters by Forty-Niners," *Frontier Guardian*, p. 110.

24. Paden, ed., *Journal of Madison Berryman Moorman*, July 26, 1850.

25. *Millennial Star* 10: 339.

26. Johnston, *Overland to California*, pp. 124–25.

27. W. Kelly, *An Excursion to California*, p. 230.

28. Williams, ed., Overland to California, p. 329.

29. W. Kelly, *An Excursion to California*, p. 230.

30. Johnston, *Overland to California*, p. 123.

31. W. Kelly, *An Excursion to California*, p. 228; John Wood, *Journal*, p. 60.

32. Johnston, *Overland to California*, pp. 123–24.

33. Early History, p. 95.

34. *Deseret News*, June 29, 1850.

35. Trowbridge, *Pioneer Days*, pp. 117–18.

36. Black, Sketch, pp. 5–8.

37. *Deseret News*, June 29, 1850; Brooks, ed., *On the Mormon Frontier* 2: 354.

38. *Deseret News,* July 20, 1850.

39. W. Kelly, *An Excursion to California,* p. 229.

40. Jewett, Diary, July 22, 1849.

41. Smucker, *History of the Mormons,* p. 315; Hoover, Diary, Aug. 19, 1849; *Millennial Star* 11: 339.

42. Clarke, Narrative, p. 8.

43. Gunnison, Journal, June 2, 1850.

44. T. Clark, ed., *Off at Sunrise,* pp. 65–66.

45. Morgan, ed., "Letters by Forty-Niners," Josselyn, p. 103; Bloom, Journal, p. 27; Udell, *Incidents of Travel,* p. 25; Bond, Diary, p. 18; Bailey, Journal of the Overland Trip, Aug 1, 1852.

46. Jewett, Diary, July 22, 1849.

47. Langworthy, *Scenery of the Plains,* p. 92.

48. McCall, *The Great California Trail,* p. 58.

49. Stansbury, *Exploration and Survey,* p. 146.

50. Hall, Diary of a Forty Niner, Aug. 1849; Ressler, ed., *Partners in the Gold Rush.*

51. Smucker, *History of the Mormons,* p. 315.

52. Stephens, *Life Sketches,* p. 15.

53. Hall, Diary of a Forty Niner, Aug. 1849.

54. Kiefer, ed., "Over Barren Plains and Rock-Bound Mountains," p. 24.

55. Stephens, *Life Sketches,* p. 15.

56. Paden, ed., *Journal of Madison Berryman Moorman,* July 21, 1850.

57. Lorton, Diary, Aug. 20, 1849.

58. Benson, Diary, p. 50.

59. Newcomb, Journal of a Trip to California, p. 117.

60. C. Ferguson, *California Gold Fields,* p. 46.

61. Trowbridge, *Pioneer Days,* p. 118.

62. Hamelin, Overland Diaries, p. 44.

63. Smucker, *History of the Mormons,* p. 316.

64. W. Taylor, "Pioneer Reminiscences," p. 3.

65. Langworthy, *Scenery of the Plains,* pp. 96–97; see also Stephens, *Life Sketches,* p. 15; Sexton, ed., *The Foster Family,* p. 45.

66. Newcomb, Journal of a Trip to California, pp. 119–20.

67. Stansbury, *Exploration and Survey,* pp. 134, 146–47.

68. Morgan, ed., "Letters by Forty-Niners, Josselyn, p. 103.

69. *Millennial Star* 11: 355–56; Early History, p. 91; *Frontier Guardian,* Sept. 5, 1849.

70. Greenwood, Journal, p. 23.

71. *Millennial Star* 11: 353.

72. Early History, p. 91.

73. Hamelin, Overland Diaries, p. 43.

74. *Millennial Star* 11: 353–59; Benson, Diary, pp. 48–50; Jesse Crosby, Journal, pp. 40–41; Early History, p. 92; Hamelin, Overland Diaries, p. 43.

75. Benson, Diary, pp. 49–50.

76. *Millennial Star* 11: 355–56; Early History, p. 92.

77. Greenwood, Journal, p. 24.

78. *Western Reserve Chronicle*, Oct. 10, 1849; W. Call, Recollections, p. 10; Darwin, Journals, p. 206.

79. Early History, p. 92.

80. C. Crosby, Journal.

81. McCall, *The Great California Trail*, p. 60.

82. Hovey, Journal, p. 197.

83. Benson, Diary, p. 51.

84. L. Brown, Journal, July 24, 1849.

85. *Millennial Star* 11: 358–59.

86. W. W. Call, Recollections, p. 10.

87. History of Brigham Young, 1850, p. 58; *Millennial Star* 12: 337–40.

88. Hudson, Papers, letter July 1850.

89. From Lake Erie to the Pacific, pp. 28–29.

90. Bloom, Journal, p. 27.

91. John Wood, *Journal*, p. 60.

92. Darwin, Journals, p. 198.

93. Hamelin, Overland Diaries, pp. 44, 56.

94. Hancock, Autobiography, p. 43.

95. Neff, *History of Utah*, pp. 556–59.

96. Wooster, *The Gold Rush*, p. 11.

97. Millington, Diary, June 4, 1850; Clay, Letter, Sept. 22, 1849.

98. W. Kelly, *An Excursion to California*, pp. 225–26.

99. Campbell and Campbell, "Pioneer Society," p. 289.

100. Langworthy, *Scenery of the Plains*, pp. 84, 94.

101. Tompkins, Diary, p. 85.

102. Senter, Letters, p. 11.

103. Johnston, *Overland to California*, p. 121.

104. DeWolf, "Diary of the Overland Trail," p. 205.

105. Ressler, ed., *Partners in the Gold Rush*; Clay, Letter, Sept. 22, 1849.

106. Stephens, *Life Sketches*, pp. 15–16.

107. J. S. Brown, *Life of a Pioneer*, p. 124.

108. Stephens, *Life Sketches*, p. 13.

109. Wylly, Westward Ho—In '49, p. 47.

110. Cook, Reminiscences and Journal, Aug. 1850.

111. From Lake Erie to the Pacific, p. 23; Wooster, *The Gold Rush*, p. 11.

112. Black, Sketch, p. 10.

113. Langworthy, *Scenery of the Plains*, pp. 100–101; Heaston, ed., *From Mississippi to California*, p. 75.

114. Clarke, Narrative, p. 9.

115. Stephens, *Life Sketches*, p. 14.

116. Ressler, ed., *Partners in the Gold Rush.*

117. Hughes, *The Life of Archibald Gardner*, p. 56.

118. Tompkins, Diary, p. 85; Langworthy, *Scenery of the Plains*, p. 94; Morgan, ed., "Letters by Forty-Niners," *Missouri Courier*, p. 113.

119. Hamelin, Overland Diaries, p. 55.

120. F. Richards, Journal, p. 85.

121. Burton, *City of the Saints*, p. 253.

122. Langworthy, *Scenery of the Plains*, p. 114.

123. Tompkins, Diary, p. 85.

124. *Western Reserve Chronicle*, Oct. 10, 1849; Hickman, *Brigham's Destroying Angel*, p. 52.

125. T. Clark, ed., *Gold Rush Diary*, p. 178.

126. Hillyer, Journal, p. 47; Hamelin, Overland Diaries, p. 50; Stephens, *Life Sketches*, p. 15.

127. Sargent, ed., *Seeking the Elephant*, pp. 154, 157.

128. W. Kelly, *An Excursion to California*, p. 225.

129. Hudson, Papers, letter July 1850; *Deseret News*, Jan. 11, 1851; C. Stuart, Trip to California, August 15, 1849; Lorton, Diary, p. 185.

130. Langworthy, *Scenery of the Plains*, p. 114.

131. S. N. Carvalho, *Incidents of Travel*, p. 158.

132. Hillyer, Journal, p. 47.

Chapter 7.   Winter Mormons

1. Miller, "Explorers and Trail Blazers," pp. 79–91; C. Kelly, "Gold Seekers on the Hastings Cutoff," pp. 3–9.

2. Read and Gaines, eds., *Gold Rush*, p. 638.

3. Hall, Diary of a Forty Niner, Sept. 1, 1849.

4. Stansbury, Journal, Nov. 1849; Stansbury, *Exploration and Survey*, pp. 111–12.

5. McDiarmid, Letters, July 28, 1850.

6. C. Kelly, "Gold Seekers on the Hastings Cutoff," pp. 13–30; see also *Millennial Star* 12: 350; C. Taylor, Diary, Aug. 14, 1850.

7. Fleming and Standing, "The Road to 'Fortune': The Salt Lake Cutoff," pp. 249–71.

8. Dundass, *Journal*, p. 42.

9. Shields, Journal, p. 114.

10. McKeeby, Memoirs, p. 30.

11. Ibid., p. 30; Wooster, *The Gold Rush*, p. 12; Johnston, *Overland to California*, p. 128; Muench, ed., *The Kilgore Journal*, p. 39.

12. Millington, Diary, June 9, 1850.

13. Langworthy, *Scenery of the Plains*, p. 117; Gunnison, Journal, May 12, 1850.

14. Lewis, Overland Diary, p. 22.

15. Shields, Journal, p. 118.

16. Kleiser, Autobiography, p. 35; Muench, ed., *The Kilgore Journal*, p. 39; Johnston, *Experiences of a Forty-niner*, p. 196.

17. Jewett, Diary, July 28, 1849; Wooster, *The Gold Rush*, p. 12; Heaston, ed., *From Mississippi to California*, p. 80; Millington, Diary, June 9, 1850; Sexton, ed., *The Foster Family*, p. 46; C. Ferguson, *California Gold Fields*, p. 50.

18. Slater, *Fruits of Mormonism*, p. 6.

19. Dundass, *Journal*, p. 43.

20. Doyle, Journals and Letters of Simon Doyle, p. 43.

21. Gould, Diary Aug. 19, 1849.

22. Heaston, ed., *From Mississippi to California*, p. 80; Sexton, ed., *The Foster Family*, p. 46.

23. Shields, Journal, p. 118; see also Sargent, ed., *Seeking the Elephant*, p. 158; Muench, ed., *The Kilgore Journal*, p. 39.

24. Babcock, Reminiscences, p. 8.

25. Throne, ed., "Documents: Letters of a Forty-niner," p. 70.

26. Senter, Letters, p. 13.

27. History of Brigham Young, 1849, p. 140; Early History, p. 98.

28. Judge H. S. Brown, Statement of Early days of Cal., p. 4.

29. Caughey, "Southwest from Salt Lake in 1849," pp. 143–70.

30. For other accounts of the companies traveling to Los Angeles in 1849, see Hafen and Hafen, eds., *Journals of Forty-niners*, pp. 15–328; Manly, *Death Valley in '49*, pp. 102–220; Lorton, Diary, pp. 1–195; Lorton, *Over the Salt Lake Trail*; Morgan, ed., "Letters by Forty-Niners," Gold Mines, p. 114; *Journal History*, Sept. 30, 1840; Bean, Autobiography, pt. 3, p. 5; Hoover, Diary, Sept. 25, 1849; Hamelin, Overland Diaries, p. 50.

31. Hafen and Hafen, eds., *Journals of Forty-Niners*, pp. 28–34; Caughey, Southwest from Salt Lake City in 1849, p. 147.

32. Hafen and Hafen, eds., *Journals of Forty-Niners*, pp. 43–44, 307.

33. Ibid., p. 44; Caughey, Southwest from Salt Lake City in 1849, pp. 157, 163.

34. Caughey, "Southwest from Salt Lake City in 1849," pp. 163–64.

35. *Millennial Star* 12: 343.

36. Wilson, Original Letters, July 29, 1850.

37. Hancock, Autobiography, p. 44.

38. Gunnison, *The Mormons*, p. 65.

39. C. Smith, Reminiscences, p. 24.

40. T. Clark, ed., *Gold Rush Diary*, p. 179.

41. Hudson, Papers, letter July 1850.

42. Madsen, ed., *A Forty-niner in Utah*, pp. 101–10.

43. Langworthy, *Scenery of the Plains*, pp. 105–7.

44. History of Brigham Young, 1850, p. 59, 88, 1849, p. 144; also see Hovey, Journal, p. 199; Journal History, Oct. 8, and Sept. 3, 1849; see also *Millennial Star* 12: 350.

45. Johnston, *Overland to California*, p. 125.

46. Benson, Diary, p. 55.

47. Thurber, Dictation, p. 2; B. Johnson, Autobiography, p. 123.

48. Black, Sketch, pp. 5–6.

49. Gunnison, Journal, May 14, 1850.

50. From Lake Erie to the Pacific, pp. 22–24.

51. Solomon Zumwalt, as quoted in Mulder and Mortensen, eds., *Among the Mormons*, p. 241; see also Zumwalt, Letter; Cook, Reminiscences and Journal, July 2, 1850.

52. Carr, *Pioneer Days in California*, pp. 46–47.

53. Hillyer, Journal, p. 47.

54. Glover, *The Mormons in California*, p. 25.

55. Jacob Y. Stover Narrative, as quoted in Caughey, "Southwest from Salt Lake in 1849," p. 169; John Smith, Papers, letter of Apr. 28, 1849; *Liverpool Mercury*, Nov. 16, 1849.

56. History of Brigham Young, 1850, p. 30.

57. Ibid.; F. Richards, Journal, pp. 5–6; Neibaur, Journal, Dec. 1, 1849.

58. *Millennial Star* 11: 340, 12: 87.

59. Morgan, ed., "Letters by Forty-Niners," *Missouri Courier*, p. 113; Sexton, ed., *The Foster Family*, p. 45.

60. Young, Diary, July 23, 25, 1849.

61. L. Brown, Journal, Oct. 24, 1850.

62. Brooks, ed., *On the Mormon Frontier* 2: 388.

63. Hudson, Papers, letter Apr. 2, 1850.

64. Gunnison, Journal, May 6, 1850.

65. Kesler, Journal, Sept. 15, 1859.

66. Brooks, ed., *On the Mormon Frontier*, 2: 386.

67. Ibid., 2: 388.

68. Ibid., p. 377.

69. Langworthy, *Scenery of the Plains*, pp. 82–117.

70. Slater, *Fruits of Mormonism*, pp. 1–94.

71. *Portland Weekly Oregonian*, Apr. 3, 10, May 1, 8, 13, 22, 29, June 12, 26, July 3, 1852.

72. Langworthy, *Scenery of the Plains*, p. 95.

73. Zumwalt, as quoted in Mulder and Mortensen, eds., *Among the Mormons*, p. 241.

74. Slater, *Fruits of Mormonism*, pp. 17–18; *Portland Weekly Oregonian*, June 12, 1852.

75. Slater, *Fruits of Mormonism*, pp. 41–58.

76. Ibid., pp. 32–36.

77. Ibid., pp. 27–29.

78. *Portland Weekly Oregonian*, May 1, 1852.

79. Slater, *Fruits of Mormonism*, pp. 67–71.

80. Brooks, ed., *On the Mormon Frontier* 2: 388.

81. L. Brown, Journal, Jan. 12, 1851.

82. *Portland Weekly Oregonian*, Apr. 3, 1852.

83. Ibid.; *Millennial Star* 15: 255.

84. Verdenal, Journal, Aug. 9, 1852.

85. Jacob, Record, p. 74.

86. *Portland Weekly Oregonian*, May 22, 1852.

87. Slater, *Fruits of Mormonism*, chap. 2; Langworthy, *Scenery of the Plains*, pp. 95–96.

88. Langworthy, *Scenery of the Plains*, pp. 95–96.

89. Slater, *Fruits of Mormonism*, p. 73 and chap. 6; also *Portland Weekly Oregonian*, May 8, 1852.

90. U.S. Congress, Report of Messrs. Brandebury, Brocchus, and Harris, pp. 88.

91. Slater, Fruits of Mormonism, pp. 15–16; Goodell, *Portland Weekly Oregonian*, May 13, 1852; Langworthy, *Scenery of the Plains*, p. 96.

92. Harrington, "Journal of Leonard E. Harrigton," p. 19.

93. Sessions, Diary, pp. 69–70.

94. *Deseret News*, July 12, 1850.

95. Brooks, ed., *On the Mormon Frontier* 2: 380–81.

96. Hudson, Papers, letter of John E. Warner to Royal E. Robbins, Mar. 8, 1852.

97. Azariah Smith, Journal, pp. 54–56.

98. Brooks, ed., *On the Mormon Frontier* 2: 393, 396.

99. Slater, *Fruits of Mormonism*, chap. 7; *Portland Weekly Oregonian*, Apr. 3, 1852; Langworthy, *Scenery, of the Plains*, pp. 96, 99–101.

100. Zumwalt, as quoted in Mulder and Mortensen, *Among the Mormons*, p. 241.

Chapter 8.   End of the Golden Rainbow

1. Mattes, *Great Platte River Road*, pp. 15–16; Myers, ed., *Ho for California!*, p. 36; Stewart, *The California Trail*, p. 232.

2. L. Brown, Journal, Mar. 29, 1851.

3. Ibid.; Heywood, *Journals*, June 15, 1851; *Deseret News*, June 14, 28, 1851; Unruh, *The Plains Across*, p. 120.

4. *Millennial Star* 12: 301.

5. *Frontier Guardian*, May 16, June 13, 1851.

6. Tracy, Life Sketch, p. 33.

7. *Deseret News*, Mar. 22, 1851; *Frontier Guardian*, May 30, 1851.

8. Keller, *A Trip Across the Plains*, p. 20.

9. L. Brown, Journal, June 28, 1851.

BIBLIOGRAPHY

Abbreviations

CSmH   Henry E. Huntington Library, San Marino, Calif.

CtY   Yale University, New Haven, Conn.

CU-B   University of California, Bancroft Library, Berkeley, Calif.

DLC   U.S. Library of Congress, Washington, D.C.

DNA   National Archives, Washington, D.C.

UHi   Utah State Historical Society, Salt Lake City, Utah

UPB   Brigham Young University, Provo, Utah

USlC   Church Historical Department, Church of Jesus Christ of Latter-day Saints, Salt Lake City, Utah

UU   University of Utah, Salt Lake City, Utah

Abbey, James. *California: A Trip Across the Plains in the Spring of 1850.* New Albany, Ind.: Kent & Norman and J. R. Nunemacher, 1850.

Adams, William. Biography, 1849. *DLC*, Manuscript Division. The Bancroft Collection of Mormon Papers. Film 55, Reel 8.

Allen, Andrew Jackson. Diary, 1849–51. *UHi*, vol. 1, item 1, Mic. A-341.

Alter, J. Cecil, ed. "The State of Deseret." *Utah Historical Quarterly* 18, nos. 2, 3, 4 (Apr., July, Oct. 1940).

Appleby, William I. Autobiography and Journal, 1850. *USlC*, MSD 1401.

Arrington, Leonard J. *Great Basin Kingdom: An Economic History of the Latter-days Saints, 1830–1900.* Cambridge: Harvard University Press, 1958. Reprint. Lincoln: University of Nebraska Press, 1966.

Arrington, Leonard J., and Davis Bitton. *The Mormon Experience: A History of the Latter-day Saints.* New York: Alfred A. Knopf, 1979.

Ashby, Robert L., ed. *Autobiography of Benjamin Ashby.* Salt Lake City: Stringham Ashby Stevens, 1941.

Ashley, Algeline Jackson. Diary: Crossing the Plains in 1852. *CSmH.*

Babcock, Leonard. Reminiscences 1849. *CU-B.*

Bailey, Mary Stuart. A Journal of the Overland Trip from Ohio to California, 1852. *CSmH.*

Bancroft, Hubert Howe. *History of California,* vol. 6, 1848–1859. San Francisco: The History Company Publishers, 1888.

[159]

————. *History of Utah*. San Francisco: The History Company Publishers, 1890.

Barry, Louise. *The Beginning of the West*. Topeka: Kansas State Historical Society, 1972.

Batchelder, Amos. Journal of a Tour Across the Continent of N. America, 1849. *CU-B*.

Bean, George Washington. Autobiography, 1849. Pt. 3. *DLC*, Manuscript Division. The Bancroft Collection of Mormon Papers. Film 48, Reel 1.

————. History, 1850. *USlC*, MSD 2142, fd. 1.

Beatie, H. S. The First in Nevada, 1849. *DLC*, Manuscript Division. The Bancroft Collection of Mormon Papers. Film 65, Reel 18.

Benson, John H. Diary, 1849. *UU*, Ms. 128.

Bieber, Ralph P. "California Gold Mania." *The Mississippi Valley Historical Review* 35. no. 1 (June 1948): 3–28.

Bitton, Davis, *Guide to Mormon Diaries and Autobiographies*. Provo, Utah: Brigham Young University Press, 1977.

Black, William Morley. Sketch of the Life of William Morley Black, 1849. *UHi*, MAN A74.

Bloom, Henry S. Journal, 1850. *UHi*, MAN A58.

Bond, Robert. Diary of Overland Trip to Great Salt Lake City, March 1st, 1849– July 17th, 1849. *CtY*.

Booth, Caleb. En Route to California, May–September, 1850. *CtY*.

Borrowman, John. Diary, 1849. *USlC*, MSD 1495, fd. 1.

Brooks, Juanita, ed. *A Mormon Chronicle: The Diaries of John D. Lee, 1848– 1876*. 2 vols. San Marino, Calif.: Henry E. Huntington Library, 1955. Reprint. Salt Lake City: University of Utah Press, 1983.

————, ed. *On the Mormon Frontier*. 2 vols. 1964. Reprint. Salt Lake City: University of Utah Press, 1982.

Brown, A. Theodore. *Frontier Community: Kansas City to 1870*. Columbia: University of Missouri Press, 1963.

Brown, James S. *Life of a Pioneer: Being the Autobiography of James S. Brown*. Salt Lake City: Geo. Q. Cannon & Sons Co., Printers, 1900.

Brown, John E. *Memoirs of a Forty-niner*. New Haven, Conn.: Associated Publishers of American Records, 1907.

Brown, Judge H. S. Statement of Early days of Cal., 1849. *CU-B*.

Brown, Lorenzo. Journal, 1849. 2 vols. *CSmH*.

Browne, George Waldo, ed. *The Gold Seekers of '49 by Kimball Webster*. Manchester, N.H.: Standard Book Company, 1917.

Bullock, Thomas. Diary, 1847. *USlC*, *Film* 803, no. 1.

Burton, Richard F. *The City of the Saints and Across the Rocky Mountains to California*. Edited by Fawn M. Brodie. New York: Alfred A. Knopf, 1963.

Bush, Charles W. Letter to "Dear Brother," Sacramento, California, Jan. 10, 1850. *CU-B*.

Call, Anson. The Life and Record of Anson Call, 1849. *CSmH*.

Call, W. W. Recollections of Overland Journey to California, 1849. *CU-B*.

Campbell, Bruce L., and Eugene E. Campbell. "Pioneer Society." In *Utah's History*, edited by Richard D. Poll, chap. 15, pp. 275–93. Provo, Utah: Brigham Young University Press, 1978.

Carr, John. *Pioneer Days in California*. Eureka, Calif.: Times Publishing Company, 1891.

Carrington, Albert. Journal. *DNA*, RG 77, Records of the Office of the Chief of Engineers, Apr. 3, 1850. Nov. 18, 1850, Cpbd. 2, Shelf 2, no. 2, File with 343.

Carruth, William. Autobiography, 1849. *USlC*, F22, no. 4.

Carter, Kate B., comp. *Life of Charles Sperry*. Salt Lake City: Daughters of Utah Pioneers, 1966.

Carvalho, S. N. *Incidents of Travel and Adventure in the Far West*. New York: Derby and Jackson, 1857.

Caughey, John W. "Southwest from Salt Lake City in 1849." *The Pacific Historical Review* 6, no. 2 (June 1937): 143–78.

Chandless, William. *A Visit to Salt Lake: Being a Journey Across the Plains*. London: Smith, Elder & Co., 1857.

Clark, Bennett C. Diary. *CtY.*

Clark, Thomas D., ed. *Gold Rush Diary: Being the Journal of Elisha Douglass Perkins on the Overland Trail in the Spring and Summer of 1849*. Lexington, Ky.: University of Kentucky Press, 1967.

————, ed. *Off at Sunrise: The Overland Journal of Charles Glass Gray*. San Marino, Calif.: Henry E. Huntington Library, 1976.

Clarke, Harriet T. Narrative, 1850. *CU-B.*

Clawson, Margaret Gay Judd. Rambling Reminiscences. *USlC*, MSD 3712, fd. 1.

Clay, Alonzo Cordell. Letter to John T. Barnett, Great Salt Lake City, Utah, Sept. 22, 1849. *CSmH.*

Coats, Felix Grundy. On the Golden Trail, 1849. *CU-B.*

Cole, Cornelius. *Memoirs of Cornelius Cole*. New York: McLoughlin Brothers, 1908.

Conover, Peter W. Autobiography, 1849–50. *UHi*, MAN A240.

Cook, Phineas W. Reminiscences and Journal, 1850–53. *USlC*, MSD 6288.

Cooke, Mrs. S. A. Theatrical and Social Affairs in Utah, 1852. *DLC*, Manuscript Division. The Bancroft Collection of Mormon Papers. Film 67, Reel 20.

Cotton, Aylett R. Across the Plains to California in 1849 and After: An Autobiography. *CU-B.*

Crane, Addison Moses. Journal, 1852. *CSmH.*

Crosby, Caroline Barnes. Journal, May 10, 1848 to Feb. 7, 1853. *UHi*, Mic. A 432, Pt 1.

Crosby, Jesse W. Journal, 1847–50. *UHi*, MAN 153–1.

Crosby, Jonathan. Autobiography, 1849. *UHi*, Mic. A 432, Pt 1.

Darwin, Charles Benjamin. Journals, notebook etc. 1849. *CSmH.*

Davies, J. Kenneth. "The Mormon Apostolic Argonauts." Paper delivered at Annual Meeting of Mormon Historical Association, May 1, 1981, Rexburg, Idaho.

DeBow, J. D. B. *Compendium of the Seventh Census of the United States.* Washington, D.C.: A.O.P. Nicholson, Public Printer, 1854.

Delano, Alonzo. *Journal.* Printed in *Weekly North-Western Gazette* (Galena, Ill.), Feb. 27, 1850.

Deseret News (Salt Lake City). 1850–51.

DeWitt, Ward G., and Florence Stark DeWitt, eds. *Prairie Schooner Lady: The Journal of Harriett Sherrill Ward, 1853.* Los Angeles: Westernlore Press, 1959.

DeWolf, David. "Diary of the Overland Trail, 1849, and Letters, 1849–1850." *Illinois State Historical Society Transactions,* no. 32, pt 3 (1925): 183–222.

Doyle, Simon. The Journals and Letters of Simon Doyle Embracing the Diaries of His Two Trips Across the Plains to California 1846-51—1854-56 and His Letters from the Diggings 1849-53 with an Account of His Return Journey via the Isthmus in 1856. *CtY.*

Duncan, Chapman. Biography, 1812–1900 (1849). *UPB,* Mss. 298.92 299, vol. 15.

Dundass, Samuel Rutherford. *Journal (1849).* Steubenville, Ohio: Printed at Conn's Job Office, 1857.

Early History. *DLC,* Manuscript Division. The Bancroft Collection of Mormon Papers. Film 77, Reel 30.

Eaton, Herbert. *The Overland Trail to California in 1852.* New York: G. P. Putnam's Sons, 1974.

Edwards, Esaias. Journal, 1849. *UHi,* PAM A176.

Ellenbecker, John G. *The . . . Jayhawkers of Death Valley.* Marysvale, Kans.: n.p., 1938.

Enos, A. A. *Personal Recollections of A. A. Enos (1850).* N.p., n.d.

Evans, James W. Journal or a Trip to California (1850). *CU-B.*

Evershed, Thomas. "The Gold Rush Journal of Thomas Evershed." *Rochester History* 39, nos. 1 and 2 (Jan. and Apr. 1977): 1–44.

Federal Writers' Project of Works Progress Administration. *Iowa: A Guide to the Hawkeye State.* New York: The Viking Press, 1938.

Ferguson, Charles. *California Gold Fields.* Oakland: Biobooks, 1948.

Ferguson, W. W. The Moving of W. W. Ferguson and Family from Owen County, Indiana and Journey to California—1849. *CU-B.*

Ferris, Benjamin G. *Utah and the Mormons.* New York: Harper & Brothers Publishers, 1856.

Fish, Joseph. Autobiography, 1849. *UU,* Ms. 34, Bx. 10, 704.

Fleming, L. A., and A. R. Standing. "The Road to 'Fortune': The Salt Lake Cutoff." *Utah Historical Quarterly* 33 no. 3 (Summer 1965): 248–71.

Flint, Dr. Thomas. *Diary of Dr. Thomas Flint, 1851–1855.* Los Angeles: Historical Society of Southern California, 1923.

Foster, Isaac. (The Foster Family). California Pioneers of 1849. *CSmH.*

Frederick, J. F. *Ben Holladay, The Stagecoach King: A Chapter in the Development of Transcontinental Transportation.* Glendale, Calif.: N.p., 1940.

Frink, Ledyard. *Journal of the Adventures of a Party of California Gold-seekers Under the Guidance of Mr. Ledyard Frink.* Oakland, Calif.: N.p., 1897.

From Lake Erie to the Pacific: An Overland Trip in 1850–51. *CSmH.*

Frontier Guardian (Kanesville, Iowa). May 1849–June 1851.

Gabriel, Ralph Henry, ed. *A Frontier Lady: Recollections of the Gold Rush and Early California by Sarah Royce.* New Haven: Yale University Press, 1932.

Gardner, Nathan Hale, ed. *Alma Helaman Hale, History & Genealogy.* Ogden, Utah: Published by author, 1961.

Giffen, Helen S., ed. *The Diaries of Peter Decker, Overland to California in 1849 and Life in the Mines, 1850–1851,* Georgetown, Calif.: The Talisman Press, 1966.

Gifford, Samuel K. Autobiography, 1850. *USlC* F44, no. 1.

Glover, William. *The Mormons in California.* Los Angeles: Glen Dawson, 1954.

Goldsmith, Oliver. *Overland in Forty-nine: The Recollections of a Wolverine Ranger after a Lapse of Forty-seven Years.* Detroit: Published by the Author, 1896.

Gould, Charles. Diary, 1849. *CU-B.*

Governor's Message; Deseret, December 2, 1850. To the Senators and Representatives of the State of Deseret. CtY.

Greenwood, William. Journal, 1822–91. *UU,* Ms. 195.

Gudde, Erwin G., ed. *Chronicle of the West; the Conquest of California, Discovery of Gold, and Mormon Settlement, as Reflected in Henry William Bigler's Diaries.* Berkeley: University of California Press, 1962.

Gunnison, Lieut. John W. Journal. *DLC,* RG 77, Records of the Office of the Chief of Engineers, Apr. 11, 1849–June 15, 1850.

———. *The Mormons, or, Latter-day Saints, in the Valley of The Great Salt Lake: A History of Their Rise and Progress, Peculiar Doctrines, Present Condition, and Prospects.* Philadelphia: Lippincott, Grambo & Co., 1852.

———. Letters, 1849–50. *CSmH.*

Hafen, LeRoy R., and Ann W. Hafen, eds. *Journals of Forty-niners: Salt Lake to Los Angeles.* Glendale, Calif.: The Arthur H. Clark Company, 1954.

Hafen, LeRoy R., ed. *The Mountain Men and the Fur Trade of the Far West.* Vol. 7. Glendale, Calif.: The Arthur H. Clark Company, 1969.

Haight, Isaac C. Diary, 1849. *DLC,* Manuscript Division. The Bancroft Collection of Mormon Papers. Film 50, Reel 3.

———. Journal, 1849. *UU,* Ms. 84.

Hale, Aroet Lucius. Journal, 1828–1911. *UU,* Acc. 556.

Hall, O. J. Diary of a Forty Niner. *CU-B.*

Hamelin, J. P., Jr. The Overland Diaries of J. P. Hamelin, Jr., 1849–50. *CtY.*

Hammond, F. A. "In Early Days: My Introduction to Mormonism." *The Juvenile Instructor* 29 (1894): 353–55, 364–69, 395–98, 463–64, 517–21.

Hancock, Mosiah Lyman. Autobiography, 1849. *UU,* Ms. 50, Bx. 52, Fd. 8.

———. Life Story, 1849. *USPC,* F47, no. 2.

Hannon, Jessie Gould, ed. *The Boston-Newton Company Venture: From Massachusetts to California in 1849.* Lincoln: University of Nebraska Press, 1969.

Hansen, Peter O. Reminiscences and Diaries, 1849. *USlC,* F330, no. 1.

Harker, Joseph. Journal, 1849. *USlC,* MSD 214.

Harmon, Appleton M. Diary, vol. 2, 1848–49. *DLC,* Manuscript Division. The Bancroft Collection of Mormon Papers. Film 51, Reel 4.

Harrington, Leonard E. "Journal of Leonard E. Harrington." *Utah Historical Quarterly* 7, no. 1 (Jan. 1940): 3–64.

Harris, Sarah Hollister. *An Unwritten Chapter of Salt Lake.* New York: Printed Privately, 1901.

Hartley, William. "Mormons, Crickets, and Gulls: A New Look at an Old Story." *Utah Historical Quarterly* 38, no. 3, (Summer 1970): 224–39.

Haun, Catherine Margaret. A Woman's Trip Across the Plains in 1849. *CSmH.*

Heaston, Michael D., ed. *From Mississippi to California: Jackson Thomason's 1849 Overland Journal.* Austin, Tex.: Jenkins Publishing Company, 1978.

Hendricks, Drusilla Dorris. "Account of Conversion." *USlC,* F555, no. 7.

Hermann, William H., ed. "Three Gold Rush Letters of Adonijah Strong Welch." *Iowa Journal of History* 57 (1959): 61–73.

Hess, John W. "John W. Hess, With the Mormon Battalion." *Utah Historical Quarterly* 4, no. 1 (Jan. 1931): 47–55.

Heward, Elizabeth (Terry). History, March, 1899. *USlC,* PFO M270.07 H597h. H597h.

Heywood, Martha S. Journals, 1851. *USlC,* F726, no. 2.

Hickman, Bill. *Brigham's Destroying Angel.* Notes by J. H. Beadle. New York: Geo. A. Crofutt, Publisher, 1872.

Hillyer, Edwin. Journal, 1849. *CtY.*

History of Brigham Young. Manuscript History of the Church, 1849–1850. *USlC.*

Hixson, Jaspar Morris. Diary, 1849. *CU-B.*

Hogan, Goudy E. History, 1849. *UPB,* Mss. M270 M82, vol. 12.

Holbrook, Joseph. History, 1849. *UHi,* MAN A80.

Holdaway, Lucinda Haws. *Biographical Sketch, 1849.* N.p., n.d.

Holzhueter, John O., ed. "From Waupun to Sacramento in 1849: The Gold Rush Journal of Edwin Hillyer." *Wisconsin Magazine of History* 49, no. 3 (Spring 1966). 210–44.

Hoover, Vincent A. Diary, 1849. *CSmH.*

Hovey, Joseph G. Journal, 1849. *USlC,* F862, no. 9.

Hudson, John. Journal, 1850. *DNA,* RG 77, Records of the Office of the Chief of Engineers, Cpbd. 34, Shelf 3.

———. Papers, Apr. 2, and July 20, 1850, dated Salt Lake City. *UU.*

Hughes, Delila Gardner. *The Life of Archibald Gardner.* West Jordan, Utah: The Archibald Gardner Family Genealogical Association, 1939.

Hulbert, Archer Butler. *Forty-niners: The Chronicle of the California Trail.* New York: Blue Ribbon Books, Inc., 1931.

Hunter, Milton R. *Brigham Young, The Colonizer.* Independence, Mo.: Zion's Printing & Publishing Company, 1945.

Hutchings, James M. Diary, 1849. *CU-B.*

Jackson, Donald Dale. *Gold Dust.* New York: Alfred A. Knopf, 1980.

Jacob, Norton. Record, 1847. *CSmH.*

Jennings, Oliver. Journal (Mar. 5–May 22, 1851). An Overland Trip from Oregon City to Vancouver & via The Columbia River & Blue Mountains to Fort Boise Fort Hall & Great Salt Lake City. *CtY.*

Jennings, William. Carson Valley, 1852. *DLC,* Manuscript Division. The Bancroft Collection of Mormon Papers. Film 65, Reel 18.

Jensen, Ross Lynn. "The Greenwood-Sublette Cutoff of the Oregon Trail." M.A. thesis, University of Utah, 1975.

Jewett, George Enoch. Diary, 1849. *CU-B.*

Johnson, Benjamin F. Autobiography, 1849–50. *USlC,* Msf 737.

Johnson, John A. Note Book, 1849. *CtY.*

Johnson, William Weber. *The Forty-niners.* New York: Time-Life Books, 1974.

Johnston, William G. *Experiences of a Forty-niner.* Pittsburgh: N.p., 1892.

———. *Overland to California.* Oakland: Biobooks, 1948.

Journal History, 1849–51. *USlC.*

Journal of Discourses. 26 vols. Liverpool, Engl.: Printed and Published by Daniel H. Wells, 1865.

Judd, Zadok Knapp. Autobiography, 1849. *UHi,* MAN A-462.

Kane, Thomas L. *The Mormons: A Discourse Delivered Before the Historical Society of Pennsylvania, March 26, 1850.* Philadelphia: King & Baird, Printers, 1850.

Keller, George. *A Trip Across the Plains and Life in California.* Massillon, Ohio: White's Press, 1851.

Kelly, Charles. "Gold Seekers on the Hastings Cutoff." *Utah Historical Quarterly* 20 (1952): 1–30.

———. *Salt Desert Trails: A History of the Hastings Cutoff.* Salt Lake City: Western Epics, 1969.

———. "The Journal of Robert Chalmers, April 13, September 1, 1850." *Utah Historical Quarterly* 20 (1952): 31–55.

Kelly, William. *Across the Rocky Mountains from New York to California: With a Visit to the Celebrated Mormon Colony, at the Great Salt Lake.* London: Simms & M'Intyre, 1852.

———. *An Excursion to California.* London: Chapman and Hall, 1851.

Kesler, Frederick. Journal. 1816–99. *UU,* 29 vols.

Kiefer, David M., ed. "Over Barren Plains and Rock-Bound Mountains: Being the Journal of a Tour by the Overland Route . . . by Adam M. Brown." *Montana Western History* 22, no. 4 (Oct. 1972): 16–29.

Kilgore, William H. *Journal.* Salt Lake City: Daughters of Utah Pioneers, Jan. 1981.

Kimball, Stanley B. *Heber C. Kimball: Mormon Patriarch and Pioneer.* Urbana: University of Illinois Press, 1981.

King, John Nevin. Journal, 1850. *CtY.*

Kleiser, James Abraham. Autobiography, 1849. *CU-B.*

Knowlton, Bryant S. "The Early History of Agriculture in Utah." M.A. thesis, University of California (Berkeley), 1941.

Korns, J. Roderic, ed. *West From Fort Bridger: The Pioneering of the Immigrant Trails Across Utah, 1846–1850.* Salt Lake City: Utah State Historical Society, 1951.

Lambert, Charles. Autobiography, 1850. *USlC,* MSD 1130.

Langworthy, Franklin. *Scenery of the Plains, Mountains, and Mines: or a Diary Kept Upon the Overland Route to California.* Ogdensburgh, N.Y.: Published by J. C. Sprague, Bookseller, Hitchcock & Tillotson, Printers, 1855.

The Latter-day Saints' Millennial Star. Edited by Orson Pratt. Liverpool, Engl.: Church of Jesus Christ of Latter-day Saints, vol. 11, 1849; vol. 12, 1850; vol. 13, 1851; vol. 15, 1853.

Laub, George. Diary, vol. 1, 1852. *UHi,* MAN A171-1

Leany, William. Autobiography, 1849. *USlC,* MSD 1011, fd. 2.

————. Life Sketch. *DLC,* Manuscript Division. The Bancroft Collection of Mormon Papers. Film 52, Reel 5.

Lewis, John F., Overland Diary, 1849. *CtY.*

Liverpool Mercury. Liverpool, Engl. May 14, 1849–June 18, 1850.

Lorton, William B. *Over the Salt Lake Trail in the Fall of '49.* Los Angeles: Privately printed, 1957.

————. Diary, 1848–50. *CU-B.*

Lund, Terry and Nora, comps. *Pulsipher Family History Book,* "History of Zerah Pulsipher, as Written by Himself," 1953. Reprinted 1963.

McArthur, Daniel D. Autobiography, 1849. *UPB,* Mss. 475.

McBride, W. S. Journal of an Overland Trip from Goshen Indiana to Salt Lake City, 1850. *CSmH.*

McCall, A. J. *The Great California Trail in 1849: Wayside Notes of an Argonaut.* Bath, N. Y.: Steuben Courier Print., 1882.

McDiarmid, Finley. Letters, 1850. *CU-B.*

McKeeby, L. C. Memoirs, 1850. *CtY.*

Madsen, Brigham D., ed. *A Forty-niner in Utah: Letters and Journal of John Hudson,* Salt Lake City: Tanner Trust Fund, University of Utah, 1981.

Manly, William Lewis. *Death Valley in '49.* Los Angeles: Borden Publishing Company, 1949.

Mattes, Merrill J., and Easley J. Kirk, eds. "From Ohio to California in 1849; The Gold Rush Journal of Elijah Bryan Farnham." *Indiana Magazine of History* 46 (Sept. and Dec. 1950): 318, 403.

Mattes, Merrill J. *The Great Platte River Road: The Covered Wagon Mainline via Fort Kearney to Fort Laramie.* Omaha: Nebraska State Historical Society, 1969.

Maynard, David Swinson. Diary of Overland Trip to Oregon, 1850. *CSmH.*

Meeks, Priddy. Journal, 1849. *UHi*, MAN 159–1.

Merkley, Christopher. *Biography of Christopher Merkley, Written by Himself.* Salt Lake City: J. H. Parry & Company, 1887 [1852].

Mighels, Ella Sterling, Comments. *How Many Miles from St. Jo?: The Log of Sterling B. F. Clark, A Forty-niner.* San Francisco: Privately Printed, 1929.

Miller, David E. "Explorers and Trail Blazers." In *Utah's History*, edited by Richard D. Poll, chap. 5, pp. 71–91. Provo, Utah: Brigham Young University -Press, 1978.

Millington, D. A. Diary, 1850–51. *CU-B*.

Moore, Arlene Mickelsen. "A Study of the Impact of the Gold Rush on the Mormon Community in Salt Lake City, 1849–1851." M.A. thesis, The American University, 1966.

Morgan, Dale L. "The Ferries of the Forty-Niners," Pt. 1. *Annals of Wyoming* 31, no. 1 (Apr. 1959): 5–31.

———. "The Ferries of the Forty-Niners." Pt. 2. *Annals of Wyoming* 31, no. 2 (Oct. 1959): 145–89.

———. "The Ferries of the Forty-Niners." Pt. 3, Sec. 1. *Annals of Wyoming* 32, no. 1 (Apr. 1960): 52–69.

———. "The Ferries of the Forty-Niners." Pt. 3, Sec. 2. *Annals of Wyoming* 32, no. 2 (Oct. 1960): 167–203.

———. *The Great Salt Lake.* Albuquerque: University of New Mexico Press, 1973.

———, ed. "Letters by Forty-Niners." *Western Humanities Review* 3, no. 2 (Apr. 1949): 98–116.

———, ed. "The Mormon Ferry on the North Platte: The Journal of William A. Empey, May 7–August 4, 1847." *Annals of Wyoming*, 21 nos. 2–3 (July–Oct. 1949): 111–67.

Morrell, Joseph R. "Medicine of the Pioneer Period in Utah." *Utah Historical Quarterly* 23, no. 2 (Apr. 1955): 127–44.

Morris, George. Autobiography, 1849. *UPB*, Man. 270.1, M832.

Muench, Joyce Rockwood, ed. *The Kilgore Journal of an Overland Journey to California in the Year 1850.* New York: Hastings House, 1949.

Mulder, William, and A. Russell Mortensen. *Among the Mormons: Historic Accounts by Contemporary Observers.* New York: Alfred A. Knopf, 1958.

Myers, Sandra L., ed. *Ho for California.* San Marino, Calif.: Henry E. Huntington Library, 1980.

Nash, Isaac B. The Life-Story of Isaac B. Nash, 1849. *UPB*, Mss. M270.1 N173.

Nebeker, John. Early Justice. *DLC*, Manuscript Division. The Bancroft Collection of Mormon Papers. Film 67, Reel 20.

Neff, Andrew Love. *History of Utah, 1847 to 1869.* Salt Lake City: The Deseret News Press, 1940.

Neibaur, Alexander. Journal, 1849. *USlC*, F72, no. 2.

Ness, Richard. Journal, 1849. *CtY*.

Newcomb, Silas. Journal of a Trip to California in 1850. *UHi*, MAN A773.

New York Times. Oct. 16, 1852.

New York Tribune. Aug 1848–July 1851.

Oregonian (Portland), June 7, 1851–July 3, 1852.

Oregon Weekly Times (Portland), June 5, 1851.

Original Manuscript Letters Written by a Family Group of Eastern Mormons while on Their Journey to Great Salt Lake City and After Their Arrival and Settlement There, 1848–56. *CtY.*

Orvis, Andrew. Journal: Wisconsin to California in 1849. *CtY.*

Paden, Irene D. *The Wake of the Prairie Schooner.* New York: The Macmillan Company, 1943.

————, ed. *The Journal of Madison Berryman Moorman, 1850–1851.* San Francisco: California Historical Society, 1948.

Parker, Dr. William Tell. Notes by the Way (1850). *CSmH.*

Pearson, Gustavus C. Recollections of a California '49er. *CU-B.*

Pettit, Edwin. *Biography of Edwin Pettit, 1834–1912.* Salt Lake City: The Arrow Press, 1933.

Poll, Richard D., ed. *Utah's History.* Provo, Utah: Brigham Young University Press, 1978.

Potter, David Morris, ed. *Trail to California: The Overland Journal of Vincent Geiger and Wakeman Bryarly.* New Haven: Yale University Press, 1945.

Porter, Rufus. *Aerial Navigation: The Practicability of Traveling Pleasantly and Safely from New-York to California in Three Days.* New York: Published by H. Smith, 1849.

Prichet, John. Notes of a Trip to California, 1849. *CU-B.*

Pulsipher, John. Diary, 1848–1850. *UHi,* MAN A928-1.

Read, Georgia Willis, and Gaines, Ruth, eds. *Gold Rush: The Journals, Drawings, and Other Papers of J. Goldsborough Bruff.* New York: Columbia University Press, 1949.

Reese, John. "Mormon Station," 1849–51. *DLC,* Manuscript Division. The Bancroft Collection of Mormon Papers. Film 65, Reel 18.

Reid, John Phillip. *Law for the Elephant: Property and Social Behavior on the Overland Trail.* San Marino, Calif.: Henry E. Huntington Library, 1980.

Ressler, Theo. C., ed. *Partners in the Gold Rush: Parallel Accounts of Two Forty-niners, Abraham Owen and John Jacob Ressler.* Williamsburg, Iowa: N.p., 1962.

Rich, Sarah Dearman Pea. Autobiography, 1849. *USlC,* MSD 1543, Rd. 2.

Richards, Franklin D. Journal, 1849–50. *USlC,* CR 100/1, Reel no. 1, vol. 13 and 14.

Richards, Jane. Reminiscences, 1850. *UHi,* MAN A221-1.

Richards, Samuel W. Journal, 1849–50. *CSmH.*

Richards, Silas. Journal, 1849. *USlC,* MSD 5030.

Roberts, Brigham H. *A Comprehensive History of the Church of Jesus Christ of Latter-day Saints,* vol. 3. Salt Lake City: Deseret News Press, 1930.

Robinson, Joseph Lee. Journal, 1849–50. *USlC,* F81, no. 2.

Sargent, Shirley, ed. *Seeking the Elephant, 1849: James Mason Hutchings' Journal of his Overland Trek to California.* Glendale, Calif.: The Arthur H. Clark Company, 1980.

Sawyer, Lorenzo. *Way Sketches: Containing Incidents of Travel Across the Plains, in 1850.* New York: Edward Eberstadt, 1926.

Scamehorn, Howard L., ed. *The Buckeye Rovers in the Gold Rush.* Athens: Ohio University Press, 1965.

Searls, Niles. Diary, 1849. Berkeley: Bancroft Library, University of California.

Senter, Riley. Letters, 1849. Berkeley: Bancroft Library, University of California.

Sessions, Patty. Diary, 1850. *UHi*, MAN A1765.

Sexton, Lucy Foster, ed. *The Foster Family: California Pioneers.* Santa Barbara: Schauer Printing Studio, Inc., 1925.

Shaw, D. A. *Eldorado, or, California as Seen By a Pioneer, 1850–1900.* Los Angeles: B. R. Baumgardt & Co., 1900.

Shields, James G. Journal of a Trip Across the Plains from Indiana to California in 1850. *CtY*.

Shinn, John R. Journal Overland from the Missouri to California, 1850. *CU-B*.

Slater, Nelson. *Fruits of Mormonism.* Coloma, Calif.: Harmon & Springer, 1851.

Smith, Albert. Reminiscences, 1850. *USlC*, MSF 814.

Smith, Azariah. Journal, 1851. *USlC*, F90, no. 2.

Smith, Charles. Reminiscences, 1849–1850. *USlC*, F410.

Smith, Jesse N. Autobiography, 1849. Salt Lake City: *USlC*, F744.

Smith, Dr. John. Journal, 1853. *CSmH*.

Smith, John. Papers, 1849. *USlC*, F 595.

Smith, John Lyman. Diary, 1849. *USlC*, MSD 2072.

————. Journal, 1850. *DLC*, Manuscript Division. The Bancroft Collection of Mormon Papers. Film 55, Reel 8.

Smoot, Margaret T. Experience of a Mormon Wife, 1849. *DLC*, Manuscript Division. The Bancroft Collection of Mormon Papers. Film 67, Reel 20.

Smucker, Samuel M., ed. *The Religious, Social, and Political History of the Mormons, or Latter-day Saints, from Their Origin to the Present Time.* New York: Hurst & Co., Publishers, 1881.

Sortore, Abram. *Biography and Early Life Sketch of the late Abram Sortore Including His Trip to California and Back.* Alexandria, Miss: N.p., Mar. 25, 1909.

Spencer, Daniel. "Biography of Daniel Spencer." *Deseret News* (Salt Lake City), Oct. 22, 1967.

Stansbury, Howard. *Exploration and Survey of the Valley of the Great Salt Lake of Utah.* Philadelphia: Lippincott, Grambo & Co., 1852.

————. Journal, 1849–50. *DNA*, RG 77, Records of the Office of the Chief of Engineers, 6 vols. June 4, 1849–Oct. 1, 1850.

Steed, Thomas. *The Life of Thomas Steed from His Own Diary, 1826–1910.* N.p., n.d.

Steele, Harriet. "Gold Rush Letters." *The Pacific Historian* (Feb. 1964): 43–52.

Stegner, Wallace. *The Gathering of Zion.* New York: McGraw-Hill Book Company, 1964.

Stephens, Lorenzo Dow. *Life Sketches of a Jayhawker of '49.* N.p., 1916.

Stewart, George R. *The California Trail.* New York: McGraw-Hill Book Company, 1962.

Storm, Colton, ed. *"A Pretty Fair View of the Eliphent," or Ten Letters by Charles G. Hinmon Written during His Trip Overland from Groveland, Illinois, to California in 1849 and His Adventures in the Gold Fields in 1849 and 1850.* Chicago: Printed for Everett D. Graff by Gordon Martin, 1960.

Street, Franklin. *California in 1850.* Also a *Concise Description of the Overland Route.* Cincinnati: R. E. Edwards & Co., 1851.

Stuart, Charles V. Trip to California, 1849. *CU-B.*

Stuart, Joseph A. *My Roving Life.* 2 vols. Auburn, Calif.: N.p., 1895.

———. Notes on a Trip to California and Life in the Mines, 1849. *CtY.*

Summers, Joseph. "Miners' and Travellers' Pocket Letter Book," 1850. New Haven: Beinecke Rare Book and Manuscript Library, Yale University.

Taylor, Calvin. Diary, Apr. 25–Sept. 4, 1850. *CU-B.*

Taylor, W. B. "Pioneer Reminiscences: Crossing the Plains in '49," printed in *Cloverdale Reveille,* Sonoma Co., Calif., Mar. 28, 1896. *CU-B.*

Thissell, G. W. *Crossing the Plains in '49.* Oakland, Calif.: N.p., 1903.

Thomas, Robert G. Historical Sketch, 1849–50. *USlC,* MSD 1598.

Throne, Mildred, ed. "Documents: Letters of a Forty-niner." *Iowa Journal of History* 47, no. 1 (Jan. 1949): 63–77.

Thurber, Albert King. A Brief Biographical Sketch, 1849. *UHi,* A5386.

Thurber, Albert King. Dictation, 1849. *DLC,* Manuscript Division. The Bancroft Collection of Mormon Papers. Film 58, Reel 11.

Tompkins, Dr. Edward Alexander. Diary: Expedition to California, 1850. *CSmH.*

Tracy, Nancy N. Life Sketch, 1852. *UHi,* MAN A502.

———. Narrative, 1852. *DLC,* Manuscript Division. The Bancroft Collection of Mormon Papers. Film 67, Reel 20.

Trowbridge, Mary Elizabeth Day, ed. *Pioneer Days: The Lifestory of Gresham and Elizabeth Day.* Philadelphia: American Baptist Publication Society, 1895.

Turnbull, T. *Travels from the United States across the Plains to California.* Madison: Published for State Historical Society of Wisconsin, 1914.

Udell, John. *Incidents of Travel to California, across The Great Plains.* Jefferson, Ohio: Printed for the Author, at the Sentinel Office, 1856.

Unruh, John D., Jr. *The Plains Across: The Overland Emigrants and the Trans-Mississippi West, 1840–60.* Urbana: University of Illinois Press, 1979.

U.S. Congress. House. *Message from the President of the United States to the Two Houses of Congress.* H. Ex. Doc. 1, 30th Cong., 2d sess., Dec. 5, 1848, p. 62.

U.S. Congress. Report of Messrs. Brandebury, Brocchus, and Harris to the President of the United States, December 19, 1851. "Speeches and Important

State Papers." *The Congressional Globe*, Appendix, vol. XXV, 32d Cong., 1st sess. Washington, D.C.: John C. Rivers, 1852.

Utah Geological and Mineralogical Survey. *Major Thermal Springs of Utah*. Water Resources Bulletin 13. Salt Lake City: University of Utah, 1970.

Utah Territorial Legislative Assembly. *Acts, Resolutions, and Memorials of the First Annual, and Special Sessions, of the Legislative Assembly of the Territory of Utah, Sept. 22, 1851*. G.S.L. City, U.T.: Brigham H. Young, Printer, 1852.

Verdenal, John M. Journal Across the Plains 1852. *CU-B*.

Ward, Margery W., ed. *A Fragment: The Autobiography of Mary Jane Mount Tanner*. Salt Lake City: Tanner Trust Fund, University of Utah Library, 1980.

Waterman, Robert Whitney. Biographical Sketch, 1850. *CU-B*.

Webb, Todd. *The Gold Rush Trail and the Road to Oregon*. Garden City, N.Y.: Doubleday & Co., Inc., 1963.

Wells, Epaphroditus. Letters, 1849. *CU-B*.

Western Reserve Chronicle (Warren, Trumbull Co., Ohio), Apr. 25, Oct. 10, 1849; Feb. 27, 1850.

Whipple, Nelson W. Autobiography, 1850. *UHi*, MAN A1429.

———. Journal, 1850. *USlC*, F279.

Whitman, A. Journal, 1850. Bks. 1 and 2. *CtY*.

Whitney, Orson F. *History of Utah*. Salt Lake City: George Q. Cannon & Sons Co., Publishers, 1892.

Widber, J. H. Statement, 1849. *CU-B*.

William, Burton J., ed. "Overland to California in 1850: The Journal of Calvin Taylor." *Utah Historical Quarterly* 38, no. 4 (Fall 1970): 312–49.

Wilson, William. Day Book, 1850. *CtY*.

———. Original Letters from the Plains and Diggings, 1850. *CtY*.

Winchell, E. C. Crossing the Plains: From the Mississippi River to the Sacramento, 1850. *CU-B*.

Winkelman, Grace. History of Provo City. *UHi*, WPA Records, Dec. 30, 1940, B57–34.

Wolcott, L. M. Diary, 1849. *CSmH*.

Wood, John. *Journal* (1850). Chillicothe, Ohio: Press of Addison Bookwalter, 1852. Reprint. Columbus, Ohio: Nevins & Myers Book and Job Printers, 1871.

Wood, Joseph Warren. Diary, 1849. vol. 1. *CSmH*.

Wooster, David. *The Gold Rush: Letters of David Wooster, from California to the Adrian, Michigan, Expositor, 1850–1855*. Mount Pleasant, Mich.: The Cumming Press, 1972.

Workers of the Writers Program, Work Projects Administration. *Provo: Pioneer Mormon City*. American Guide Series. Portland, Ore. Binfords & Mort, Publishers, 1942.

Wylly, Thomas S. Westward Ho—In '49: Memoirs of Captain Thomas S. Wylly. *CU-B*.

Wyman, Walker D., ed. *California Emigrant Letters*. New York: Bookman Associates, Publishers, 1952.

Young, Sheldon. Diary—from Joliet, Illinois to Rancho San Francisquito, California (A Jayhawker—Mar. 18, 1849– Feb. 5, 1850). *CSmH*.

Zumwalt, Solomon. Letter to *Oregonian*, Mohawk, Lane Co., Oregon, Apr. 27, 1887. *CSmH*.

INDEX